HAPPYDOG
HAPPYYOU

*Quick Tips for Building a Bond
with Your Furry Friend*

ARDEN MOORE

Storey

The mission of Storey Publishing is to serve our customers by publishing practical information that encourages personal independence in harmony with the environment.

Edited by Lisa H. Hiley
Art direction by Alethea Morrison
Cover and book design by Jessica Hische
Indexed by Nancy D. Wood

Text © 2008 by Arden Moore
Illustrations © by Jessica Hische

Printed in the United States by R.R. Donnelley
10 9 8 7 6 5 4 3 2 1

Library of Congress Cataloging-in-Publication Data

Moore, Arden.
  Happy dog, happy you / Arden Moore.
    p. cm.
  Rev. ed. of: 50 simple ways to pamper your dog. c2000.
  Includes index.
  ISBN 978-1-60342-032-7 (pbk. : alk. paper)
  1. Dogs. I. Moore, Arden. 50 simple ways to pamper your dog. II. Title.
SF426.M676 2008
636.7—dc22

                                          2008022428

To my dandy doggy duo, Chipper and Cleo,
and all the dogs who unleash joy and
laughter in our lives.

ACKNOWLEDGMENTS

I extend big tail wags of gratitude to all the veterinarians, animal behaviorists, dog trainers, and pet lovers who generously shared their ideas with me to make this planet a much better place for our canine pals. Special thanks to my editor, Lisa Hiley, for bringing out the very best in these pages.

CONTENTS

. . . .

I define joy as hearing a happy tail thumping. Witnessing a full body wiggle. Being the lucky recipient of a big, sloppy kiss.

Each and every day, our dogs shower us with gratitude, kindness, and a dash of playfulness. They lick off our tears, dance in our delight, and snuggle when we need a hug. Quite simply, dogs enhance our lives. They bring out the fun kid in all of us.

Paw through these pages and you will discover hundreds of ways to celebrate that wonderful connection you have with your canine pal. Learn how to turn ho-hum walks into mini-adventures and how to unleash your true party animal. Discover the joy of road trips and learn how to become a canine chef.

Don't feel guilty about having limited time to spend with your dog. Make the most of the time you have. This book is filled with simple, easy tips designed to truly make it a dog's life.

Got woof? Consider yourself doggone lucky. I do every day.

Paws Up!

Arden Moore

Bringing Out the Doggone Best in Both of You

Chapter One

HAPPY DOG
HAPPY YOU

....

THERE IS SOMETHING MAGICAL, MYSTERIOUS, AND DOWNRIGHT MISCHIEVOUS ABOUT DOGS. We know all too well that they love to lick, but just what makes that tail-wagger tick? What goes on inside that canine mind? Here's a clue: Dogs need to know where they rank in the family. They will be content to rank dead last — even behind the gerbil — as long as you consistently act like the leader of the pack. Most dogs just want to feel secure in their pack structure.

Here are some ways to help your dog view you as a benevolent leader, not a barking bully, and bring out the joy in both of you.

....

Dogs come in all sizes, shapes, and temperaments. The 150+ breeds recognized by the American Kennel Club range in size from teacup to linebacker. Some breeds — such as corgis and collies — have been genetically engineered to herd, while others — such as beagles and bloodhounds — are geared to be supreme sniffers. Although there are plenty of exceptions within breeds, a Labrador retriever is far more likely in general to jump into a lake after a tossed tennis ball than is a Japanese chin who prefers snuggling in your lap to swimming laps.

BASIC TRAINING

....

The best way to make your dog happy and content is to give him a clear idea of your house rules. Basic obedience training is the foundation of your relationship with your dog, but there's no need to act like Moses and bark out doggy commandments from the mountaintop. Instead, practice the three Cs: Be clear, consistent, and concise in your training. Remember, you can't play games unless your dog has learned some obedience.

Every dog should know some basic canine manners in order to be a fully functioning member of the family who is a pleasure to have around:

Come. Even if it means abandoning a rabbit chase. Be sure to praise your dog each time to reinforce the importance of this cue.

Sit. Dogs who master this fundamental are less likely to rush out an open door, fight with other dogs, or jump on guests.

Stay. Your dog should not move or stand up, but grinning and tail wagging are permitted.

Off. This instructs dogs to stop jumping on people or to vacate the furniture — *pronto*.

Heel. (Or you can ask your dog to "walk nicely.") It's safer and more pleasant to have a dog who walks politely next to you than one who lunges and tugs at the leash.

Drop it. (Or "leave it.") It's important that your dog promptly obey your request to give up a prized shoe or a potentially dangerous object.

Go to bed. (Or "find your spot.") This means it's time to head for his sleeping place for some quiet time.

Stand. This makes chores such as grooming, bathing, wiping off muddy paws, and plucking out burrs faster and easier for both of you.

Yes. This magic word tells your dog that you are pleased with his behavior and aware that he is acting like an angel.

TERRIFIC TIP

If Fido is up to mischief, practice
redirection instead of yelling at
him. Call his name to focus his
attention on you. Then ask him
for a more appropriate behavior
("Come!" or "Sit!") and reward
his good behavior.

Playtime provides a safe mental and physical outlet for both dog and owner. Playing together reduces stress, improves cardiovascular health, and lessens doggy misdeeds such as chewing, excessive barking, and digging.

Playing with your dog also makes him more accepting of your touch. Just a few minutes of romping in the backyard, a quick game of fetch or tug-of-war in the family room, or a short walk around the block will strengthen your bond with your dog.

A MENSA MOMENT

....

Test your dog's IQ by playing blanket peek-a-boo. Have your dog stand. Then drape a small blanket over his head, covering his eyes. Time how long it takes him to shake off the blanket. Brainy dogs figure it out within 15 seconds.

Note: The standing position is the key to this brain-teaser — a smart but prone canine might be quite happy to snooze under the blanket rather than rid himself of it.

Reinforce commands during training sessions with tiny pieces of treats. The small size is easy to chew and swallow quickly, and little treats won't cause major weight gain. After each gulp, your dog will be eager for another and more motivated to pay attention and respond to your next request.

Dogs are creatures of habit, so stick to a routine as much as possible. Try to feed your dog at the same time each day and take her on walks at scheduled times. A consistent household routine helps your dog to feel more secure.

Limit your training sessions to 20 minutes maximum. Dogs have short attention spans and need to shift their energies elsewhere after a session of concentrated learning. Even better is to spend 5 to 10 minutes twice a day on training sessions. Be sure to end each session on a positive note — after your dog successfully masters a trick or responds to a cue — rather than ending on a sour note. You can even go back to a familiar old trick if your dog hasn't mastered the new one yet. Stop before your dog shows signs of distraction or boredom.

TERRIFIC TIP

Mix your usual rewards with an occasional premium treat, such as a small chunk of cheese or a bit of dried liver. This reinforces the idea that being obedient can pay off big time!

PLAYING *by the* RULES

....

Always be the one to initiate and end an activity — especially games like tug-of-war, which can turn into a dominance issue. This one is best played by people with doggy confidence and control. Dogs must learn that they can latch onto an object only when you offer it to them. They must also learn to let go when you say so. If your dog accidentally nips you, end the game immediately. He will learn to tone down his intensity the next time you play.

As cute as puppies are, they must be taught how to socialize. While most people don't bring home a puppy until he is 8 to 10 weeks of age (12 weeks is ideal), the prime learning time is between 4 and 14 weeks of age. This age is the golden opportunity for the puppy's breeder or foster parent to instill good manners, self-confidence, and trust in the newest addition to a family.

During this time, it is vital to expose an impressionable puppy to nonaggressive dogs, big dogs, little dogs, happy dogs, and playful dogs — make sure they are all up-to-date on their vaccinations. He should meet tall people, short people, old people, and young people. Introduce him to people who speak with accents and those who wear hats. And yes, he should even meet a few c-a-t-s!

A puppy needs to become accustomed to his surroundings early on so that he doesn't develop unfounded fears. During that "golden year" of puppy-hood, expose him to sounds of the vacuum cleaner, the dishwasher, the dryer, and the lawn mower. Introduce him to his reflection in mirrors. Help him to feel comfortable on different surfaces and at different heights. Hoist him up onto the slick dryer top (the surface simulates a veterinary clinic's exam table) and walk him across grass, gravel, and pavement, as well as up and down stairs. As his self-confidence builds, his trust in you deepens and you both win.

Use both hands to pick up your puppy or pint-size dog. Place one hand under his chest just behind his forelegs. Put the other hand under his belly. Lift and cradle his hind legs in one arm and let his forelegs rest on your other arm for comfort and support and to prevent him from squirming, falling, and possibly injuring himself.

Make your hand a friend to your dog. If you hit or grab her, she will learn to mistrust hands and may become fear-aggressive.

Don't pat your dog on the head, which can be intimidating and uncomfortable. *Thump, thump, thump.* Not very inviting, is it? Most dogs prefer to be scratched around the ears, on the throat and chin, and at the base of the tail. Long, sweeping strokes along the back will also be appreciated.

TERRIFIC TIP

Incorporate basic obedience commands into everyday situations. If your dog loves fetching a Frisbee, ask him to sit or lie down before you toss it. When you blend basic commands into play, your dog is more likely to obey.

CAN YOU DIG IT?

....

Some dogs just have to dig. It's in their genetic makeup. Divert damage away from your prized petunias by dedicating a place in your backyard for that "dig-gone dog." Build him his own sandbox. Depending on the size of the dog and your backyard, a 3- or 4-foot-square area would be just dandy.

1. Choose a flat area in your backyard, preferably away from your gardens.

2. Remove the sod and dig down at least 18 inches. Remove the dirt, yank out the roots, and pluck out rocks and other debris.

3. Fill the hole with sand or soft dirt.

4. Introduce your dog to his new "digs" by tossing some treats on top. Praise him when he finds them.

5. Tuck more treats a couple of inches under the sand and encourage him to dig for buried treasure. You can also bury your dog's favorite toy and tell him to go find it.

6. If he strays back to your garden, tell him "no" and redirect him to his sandbox with a toy or treat. He will soon learn that there are more perks and prizes in his sandbox than in your garden plots.

What do you do with a yapping dog? Try rewarding him for silence. If you shout when your dog goes on a barking spree, he will think that you are joining in the fun or helping to spread the alarm.

Dogs quickly realize that barking is a great ploy for attention. Rather than yelling when your dog barks at a  passerby, call him to you and make him sit and wait quietly for a treat. Praise him calmly but warmly when he is doing his best mime impression.

COMMON "CENTS"

. . . .

Stop a vocalizing dog in midbark with this trick: Put a handful of pennies into a rinsed soda can and seal the opening with duct tape. The next time your dog goes on a yapping spree, say, "hush" and give the can a few vigorous shakes or toss it so that it lands near him (without hitting him, of course). The noise should startle him enough to silence him. Then call him over and make him sit or do a trick for a reward.

TERRIFIC TIP

It's always easier and more pleasant for both of you if you look for opportunities to reinforce desirable behavior instead of punishing unwanted behavior. No one — or, that is, no dog — likes to feel that he is constantly "in the doghouse."

"Bad" behavior often stems from boredom and lack of exercise, so exercise your pal often with brisk, long walks and intense play sessions. This will tucker him out and make him want to sleep rather than bark at passersby, chew on your belongings, or chase the cat.

CRANK *DOWN the* VOLUME

....

Respect your dog's keen senses — especially his ability to hear at least five times better than you can. If you want to crank up the volume, use headphones or make sure your dog can slip off to another room or hang out in a safe, enclosed backyard.

Be sensitive to the volume while you're both in the car, too; headphones aren't a good idea for the driver, and your dog has no way to move out of range of the car speakers.

Concentrate on reading and understanding your dog's body language and the signals of other dogs you meet. For example, happy, contented dogs tend to show relaxed facial muscles, open-mouthed grins, circular tail wags, and full-body wiggles. Play-bowing (chest down, front legs extended, back end up, and tail wagging) is the universal canine sign for "Let's play!" Tight lips, a direct stare, and a stiff-legged stance, however, are warnings to steer clear.

WHAT'S *in a* KISS?

....

It's okay to accept a sloppy kiss from your dog — she is showering you with affection and respect. This is the canine equivalent of sending you roses and acknowledging that you rock her world. In dog-to-dog "conversations," a dog will gently kiss the muzzle of another dog as a way to accept that the kissed dog ranks higher on the canine hierarchy.

If you don't care for canine caresses, teach her to give you her paw or rest her head in your lap as a token of affection instead of slobbering all over you.

Bowwow Bonding:
*Becoming a Better Buddy
to Your Dog*

HAPPY DOG
HAPPY YO[U]

Chapter
Two

. . . .

AND THE LATEST PET SURVEY SAYS . . . 90 PERCENT OF PEOPLE REGARD THEIR DOGS AS MEMBERS of their family. That's grrr-eat, but we need to work on the other 10 percent and convince them how doggone lucky they are to share their lives with mankind's best friend.

Let's face it: Dogs bring out the best in us. They elevate our moods. They remind us how to live in the moment. Many of us count our dogs among our best, most trusted friends. It's a two-way street, this people–dog partnership. Here are some ways for you to bolster this special bond.

. . . .

When you feel down or stressed, call your dog over and tell her your problems. Dogs are wonderful listeners and have a naturally calming influence. They can help people to cope with feelings of frustration and isolation. Researchers from leading hospitals confirm that dogs do a body good — mentally and physically. Studies have shown that patting a dog can lower blood pressure and reduce stress in humans. Some psychologists employ calm, loving canines in their practices to help their patients to address emotional issues.

Practice showing the same unconditional love for your dog that she showers on you. Pamper her with cuddling, friendly chatting, and playing. Obviously you can't spend all your time focused on your dog, but try giving her some undivided attention in 5-minute spurts throughout the day. Here are five quick ideas for building your bond:

- Work on a new trick, like having her balance a biscuit on her nose or roll over and play possum.

- Reinforce basic obedience commands every day.

- While you groom your dog's coat, run your fingers over her body to look for suspicious bumps, lumps, or cuts.

- Play hide-and-seek or another fun game in the house with your dog.

- Sing and dance with your dog to a favorite song. A little silliness will put both of you in a good mood.

TAIL-WAGGIN' TALES

....

Love to talk about your dog? Go ahead and tell your friends about a funny antic or a cool trick that he's just perfected. It feels good to brag a bit, and with all the stress we face these days, people deserve to hear some upbeat news.

Likewise, be a good listener to others who wish to share a doggone good tale about their canine pal. And if your listener's eyes start to glaze over, you might try barking up another tree!

Your dog may never reign as a Scrabble champ, but don't underestimate her word power. Dogs can comprehend up to 100 words, from *treat* to *fetch*. Be creative with your vocabulary-building lessons for your dog. If you speak clearly and perhaps use hand signals, your dog can learn to distinguish *bath* from *bark* and *snack* from *snake*.

TAKE *a* BREAK

....

Hours can zip by easily when you are plowing through paperwork or working on a must-do home project. Dogs seem to know when we need a break and will often paw our leg or let out a little yip. When you find yourself with a pile of office work at home, don't forget to take a "Bowser break" and play with your dog for a few minutes or take him for a short walk. Chances are you will be in a better mood and able to focus better because of it.

SMOOCH YOUR POOCH

....

Take some time every day to interact with your
dog on a purely emotional level. A national study
conducted by the American Pet Product Manufacturers Association reports that, on average, dog
owners show affection to their dogs 11 times a day.
A quick pat or stroke, a scratch behind the ears, or
a kiss on the nose is always appreciated. Be aware,
however, that many dogs are uncomfortable with
being hugged — it can feel too confining or even a
bit threatening.

Unleash your affection for your dog. When your dog is sitting nicely and sends a soft-eyed look your way, take your open palm and touch your chest and then touch his chest as you say, "From my heart to yours, I love you." This is a "Howl-mark" moment that your dog will feel and embrace.

BOWWOW BOWLING

....

Stage an impromptu game of canine bowling:

- Ask your dog to lie down and stay.

- Standing directly in front of him, roll a small treat between his front paws and have him leave the treat until you say "okay" so he knows he can gobble it down.

- Do this several times and then step back and test your bowling skills even further.

- If your aim is off and the treat lands outside your dog's paws, tell him to "leave it" or reinforce the "stay" cue.

- Quickly move to your dog and drop him an extra tasty treat as a reward for leaving the first one alone.

This game may take some practice, but it will pay off when you need your dog to hold a down and stay despite distractions.

TERRIFIC TIP

Unlike cats, dogs can't see very well at night. In the winter, it can be pitch black by the time you come home from work, so put a couple of lights on timers so your dog isn't left in the dark.

WHAT'S THAT YOU SAY?

·····················

When people meet, they exchange handshakes and say, "Hi, how are you doing?" When two dogs meet, they sniff each other. Same idea — different approach. While we do read body language (waving, offering a hand, smiling), we rely primarily on the spoken word; dogs depend almost completely on scents and body posture cues.

To bridge this communication gap and truly talk to dogs, you need to learn Dogspeak. Dogs have a rich "vocabulary" that consists of body language, vocal sounds, eye contact, and behavior. So don't just listen to your dog's bark. You'll understand his true message when you factor in body cues.

Use these translation tips to keep yourself from committing a furry faux pas:

- Dogs respond to intonations and body language, so pay careful attention to your tone of voice. "Good boy" spoken in a harsh, low tone will be mistaken for a scolding by your dog.

- Become a better "listener" by recognizing your dog's usual habits and expressions. Circular tail-wagging is a friendly invitation to play between most dogs, whereas side-to-side wagging could be either a welcome sign or a warning to back away.

- Avoid direct eye contact when first meeting a dog — especially one who seems worried, high-strung, or aggressive. Staring can be misinterpreted as a threat or challenge. Instead, turn slightly away from the dog until he feels more comfortable with your company.

- Accept true dog affection. A dog who licks your face is saying "I love you" in Dogspeak. When he flops at your feet with a sweet, soft-eyed look and a wide-mouthed grin, he is signaling that you rock his world.

FOUL WEATHER FIDO

....

Neither rain nor sleet nor steamy heat should prevent a dog from engaging in daily play and exercise. When the weather is anything but fetching, play indoors.

How about a canine treasure hunt? Put your dog in a stay and show him a treat. Then place the treat behind a chair while your dog watches you. Go back to him and say, "Find the treasure." Once your dog understands the concept, pretend to stash treats in several places in a room, but leave the treasure in only one location. Then tell him to "find the treasure." Praise him when he discovers his tasty prize.

GOING "IN-DOG-NITO"

....

Encourage your dog to be a master of disguise by making it fun for him to don a hat or sunglasses. This trick is designed not only to wow your friends but also to teach your dog not to make a big deal out of having something on his face or head. Start by putting your dog in a sit/stay. Allow him to sniff and inspect the hat or glasses before you touch them to his head. Praise and give a small treat.

Do this a few times, keeping the item on his head a few seconds longer each time. Then have him actually wear the hat or sunglasses for a second, praise, treat, and remove it. Slowly extend the time your dog wears the item before you hand over a treat.

If he's not enjoying the game, don't persist. Try again another day or find another way to have fun together.

"Snoopy Says" is a fun indoor game that you can play with dogs and kids. The goal is for all two- and four-legged contestants to heed your "Snoopy Says" requests to sit, stand, circle, or plop down. It's a quick and fun way to reinforce good doggy manners and is sure to bring out the giggles in your kids.

Strengthen your dog's connection with everyone in your household by playing "Find the Person." Start by having one person — say her name is Flo — hold a favorite toy. Touch the person and say her name. Next, with a treat in your hand, guide your dog toward the person as you say, "Find Flo." Treat and praise him when he does so. Once your dog is consistently finding a person in the same room, have the person take the toy and dash out of view and then ask your dog to find her.

Once your dog does this a few times, introduce another family member who may be named, say, Randy. Tell your dog to "find Randy." With practice, your dog will know names well enough to go to everyone on cue.

For your well-behaved dog who deserves to come and go between your house and your enclosed yard during balmy days, you might consider installing an instant pet screen in your back door. It allows dogs to walk through and closes automatically behind them to stop unwanted bugs from buzzing into your home. It can be installed in minutes without damaging your doorframe.

Cool your heels and your dog's paws by treating her to a canine pad that contains a cooling nontoxic gel. Tiles are cool, for sure, but they can take a toll on a dog's joints.

When the weather gets chilly, spoil your dog with a heated bed to snuggle down on (just make sure the heating element is safe from chewing). A warm bed or one made of memory foam will provide true creature comfort to your senior or arthritic dog.

All types of fancy doggy beds are available from a variety of pet and canine suppliers. Most come in a variety of colors and are easy to clean.

Music has clearly gone to the dogs ever since Elvis sang "You Ain't Nothin' but a Hound Dog." Treat your home-alone dog to CDs featuring songs fit for a dog. You can set your CD player so that it continuously plays a selection of made-for-dogs tunes during the day. Having music or a radio playing softly can help calm an anxious dog by muting irritating or distracting outside noise.

TERRIFIC TIP

Dogs look to us for clear direction and guidance. Display an air of confidence. Don't be wishy-washy or deliver conflicting orders. No one needs canine confusion.

MAKE 'EM LAUGH

....

You can always bring out the joy in your dogs by speaking in a happy voice with an upbeat tone — and if you are feeling grumpy, you might even begin to feel a bit more gleeful yourself.

Try letting out a few hearty "HEE HEEs" and "HA HAs" to boost your mood and your dog's. Your dog will have no idea what triggered your laugh track, but he will definitely pick up on your animated mood and want to play or do a dance. Be spontaneous.

I sometimes start laughing when I walk up the stairs or return inside after fetching my mail. The sound of my giggles brings out the goofy nature in my dogs, Chipper and Cleo, who come running with big grins and happy wags.

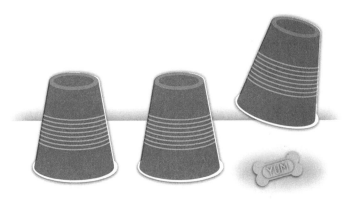

Teach your dog to behave like a Houdini hound. Hold a small treat or ball in one closed fist and keep the other fist empty. Extend both arms in front of you and ask your dog, "Which hand?" Let him sniff both. When he noses or paws at the fist with the toy or food, open it, show him, and praise him. Repeat, randomly moving the toy or food into your left or right hand. Now you're both ready for an audience!

FROM *the* MOUTHS *of* DOGS

....

Most of us fill our days meeting work deadlines, maneuvering in traffic, and doing chores. What are priorities among canines? Here are some ways in which dogs can tutor us on life:

- Run, romp, and play daily.

- If you want what lies buried, dig until you find it.

- When you're happy, dance around and wag your entire body.

- When it's in your best interest, practice obedience.

- Never pass up the opportunity to go for a joyride.

- Take naps and stretch before rising.

(Author unknown.)

STORY TIME

....

Invite your dog to join you on the sofa or on the bed when you read the newspaper or a chapter from a favorite novel. Read out loud. Your dog doesn't care that the Chicago Bears just beat the Green Bay Packers or how the stock market is faring. He just enjoys the sound of your voice and the companionship of having you nearby.

Prefer that your dogs not lounge about on the furniture? Then join them on the floor with comfy pillows or a beanbag-type chair.

TERRIFIC TIP

Deliver plenty of verbal praise in an upbeat voice: "You're a great dog — a truly great dog." Remember to include your dog's name to reinforce this positive message.

PUTTING *on the* DOG

....

Participate in events in your community that spotlight dogs. These may include pet walkathons or other animal-related fund-raisers, local parades, just-for-fun pet shows, or Bark in the Park days during which dogs can be treated to massages, dog portraits, and fun games, such as musical chairs. Invite your friends with sweet-tempered dogs to join you and make a dog day of it.

One of our favorite annual events is a dog walk held for a local animal shelter. My two dogs and I raise pledges from our friends to benefit homeless pets and we enjoy the two-mile walk. The trek takes us past a horse farm where Chipper and Cleo get a chance to sniff and eye these hay-eaters up close. Talk about horsing around!

For the TV-viewing dog, rent tail-wagging favorites from your video store. Not sure where to start? Try these canine classics:

- *101 Dalmatians*
- *The Adventures of Milo and Otis*
- *Because of Winn-Dixie*
- *Beethoven*
- *Benji*
- *Homeward Bound: The Incredible Journey*
- *Lassie, Come Home*
- *My Dog Skip*

You can also record pet shows on television and watch them later with your furry friend.

SUGAR PIE, HONEY BUNCH

·················

Give your dog a pet name or two, or three. My dog Chipper also answers to Torpedo Nose and Chipper-licious. Cleo, my other dog, responds happily to Terrier Tough and Mini-Dog. Just like us, dogs seem to welcome nicknames — they can sense the affection behind them. Even in fun, though, avoid calling your dog "stupid" or "dumbo." Those negative terms can't help affecting your outlook.

PICTURE THIS!

. . . .

Splurge on a professional photo session with you and your marvelous mutt or pleasing pure-bred. Your dog may not appreciate or understand the photos themselves, but she will most certainly welcome the added attention she receives during the photo shoot. Frame the best images for your walls or load up one of those nifty frames that feature a computerized slide show. Use your favorite shot to customize your holiday cards, signed with your dog's paw print.

In the Doghouse: *Making Your Home Fit for Fido*

Chapter Three

HAPPY DOG
HAPPY YOU

······································

YOU CAN MAKE YOUR HOME INTO YOUR DOG'S CASTLE WITHOUT GOING TO A LOT OF TROUBLE or expense. When you think about it, most dogs spend more time inside the house than the rest of the family does, so they deserve some pup-pleasing décor perks and dog-friendly conveniences. With a little imagination and insight, you can add a touch of *fang shui* to your home without feeling as if your place has totally gone to the dogs.

······································

Keep your dog's playthings stashed in a small toy chest or a pretty basket. Bring out a few at a time to keep your dog occupied but not overwhelmed by the selection. By rotating her toys so that she doesn't tire of them, you can renew a sense of excitement in your dog. (*Wow! I thought that toy squirrel was lost for good.*) This tactic also saves you some money at the pet supply store. Everyone wins!

TERRIFIC TIP

Strategically scatter some comfy
no-skid rugs on hardwood or tile
floors to cushion the pressure
points of napping dogs.

You've heard the expression, "nosy Nelly," right? With dogs, it's all about the nose. To keep your dog from becoming bored while you're away, let him sniff out — and see and hear — what's happening in your neighborhood by opening the blinds and curtains to allow warm sunshine to pour in and to provide a good lookout spot for watching what's going on outside. Cater to your home-alone canine even more by opening a window a bit to let in the outside air filled with olfactory delights.

Do this only if the window is secure and your dog can't pull a "Houdini hound" maneuver and escape. Also, if your dog is prone to barking at everything he sees, choose a window at the back of the house and avoid making him an unpopular neighbor.

Why should cats be the only pets with indoor bathroom privileges? One of the newest canine creations is the doggy litter box! It is ideal for house-training a puppy or providing relief for a senior dog with a weak bladder.

One of my favorite versions is a nifty portable dog potty pad complete with faux grass. It looks and feels like real grass but has an organic attractant that motivates dogs to "do their business" on the grass and not on your rug. It's easy to clean, and it can also be used for outside balconies and on boats — making a true "poop" deck!

Take away tasty temptations like last night's pot roast plate scrapings by stashing kitchen garbage in heavy-lidded containers or inside a latched cabinet. Digging through the garbage creates a cleanup hassle for you, and provides Fido the opportunity to give himself quite a bellyache from gobbling leftovers. I keep my covered kitchen trash can inside my pantry. The lid keeps odors sealed inside the can, and the pantry door keeps my dogs from trashing the place.

CRATE, SWEET CRATE

....

Crate-training can make a huge difference in your dog's behavior and your peace of mind when you cannot be around to safely supervise him. Think of the crate as a haven for comfort or privacy rather than a temporary prison for misbehavior. Your dog should view it as a safe, friendly place in which to sleep and spend time when you aren't around.

When you are at home, leave the crate door open so that he can come and go at will. When you do have to leave him, make sure to provide a couple of favorite toys and a bowl of water.

Never keep your dog in a crate during the day for longer than six or seven hours. It's too confining, not to mention too much of a bladder challenge. For times when you need to be gone for eight or ten hours, arrange for a pet sitter or trusted neighbor to walk your dog in the middle of the day.

Here are some ways to set your dog up with a comfortable, secure crate:

- Invest in a quality, well-designed crate that you won't have to replace because the door breaks or the metal rusts or the bars bend.

- Bigger is not better when it comes to housebreaking. Choose a crate that is just big enough to allow your dog to stand up straight, turn around, and lie down. (You can use a removable barrier to keep the space cozy while your puppy grows to his full size.)

- Put the crate in an area with good air circulation but no drafts or breezes.

- Insert a soft pet bed or thick cushion on the bottom of the crate. (If your puppy chews up his first bed, try a pile of old towels or blankets until he stops teething.)

Could you nickname your dog Sir Shed-a-Lot? Some breeds, such as beagles, have spiky hair that lodges in fabric and can be as stubborn as — yes, you guessed it — a hound to remove. Tape rollers work for clothing, but you can also find products designed to remove large amounts of hair at once; they come in sheets.

If your dog is allowed on the furniture, you can drape throw blankets or cotton sheets over sofas and recliners so he can snooze without depositing a mountain of hair on your upholstery. Be sure the sheet or blanket is big enough to cover the furniture's arms, which are perfect snooze spots for drooling dogs!

Dogs are social animals and don't like isolation. You won't often find a *Grrrr-eta Garbo* in the canine world who declares, *"I vant to be alone."* Place a dog bed in a quiet spot near a busy area of your home, such as a corner of the kitchen or living room. The bed is a refuge where your dog can be out of the way, but it also keeps her within sight of family activities.

Practice common cents by picking up pennies that are within reach of dogs. All pennies minted after 1982 contain a high zinc concentration that can be poisonous to a dog if swallowed. Believe it or not, dogs will eat all kinds of items!

TERRIFIC TIP

Cut a piece of soft fleece material to fit the size of the crate floor and place it on top of the cushion. Keep several on hand so that you can toss a dirty one into the wash and replace it right away.

THE INS *and* OUTS *of* DOG DOORS

....

If you have an enclosed backyard, free yourself from doorman duty! Give your well-behaved dog some freedom of movement by installing a dog door. Your dog will be free to come and go, even when you're not around.

Dog doors help in the behavior department, too. If your dog learns to use a pet door, he will be less apt to chew destructively or dig to release stress. The same goes for excessive barking, door-scratching, or accidental puddles inside the house. Just make sure the outside area is safe with a fence or other structure that keeps your dog from escaping.

COMING *and* GOING

....

There are many door designs that can be installed in existing doors or walls. Some can be set up as separate panels that act as extensions to sliding glass doors.

A plastic-flap style works well in mild climates. If you use the plastic-flap style, make sure it is flexible, safe, and nontoxic.

Determine which locking system works best for you and your dog: magnetic, latching, or electronic. Your dog can be fitted with an electronic collar that permits only her to have access, preventing other neighborhood pets — or even a curious raccoon — from stopping by for an unannounced visit.

Build up your dog's confidence by leaving the flap or door off at first. Have someone stay inside with your dog while you go outside. Call your dog through the hole, praise him lavishly, and give him a food treat. Once he has the hang of it, add the door and follow the same steps.

Check your puppy's collar frequently as he grows to make sure that it continues to fit him. Or provide him with an expandable one that won't cut into his skin as he grows.

Consider harnesses instead of collars for pint-size dogs. Those little guys may act like big dogs, but their necks are no match for leash-yanking.

IT'S SHOCKING!

....

A bored dog or teething pup will chew on just about anything. Be safe by looking for lamps and appliances with electrical safety cords that prevent shocks or sparks if gnawed on. Try dusting electrical cords with cayenne pepper or a commercial repellent (available at pet supply stores) to discourage chewing. Or you can house the cords in sturdy casing (available at hardware stores).

TERRIFIC TIP

Offer a portion of your dog's meal calories in the form of rewards during training sessions or as treats for doing tricks. Give small pieces rather than large ones, and limit the number in a day.

Don't panic if you catch your dog occasionally taking a drink out of your (presumably) clean toilet bowl. Dogs may not discriminate between "eau de toilet" and the finest spring water, but stainless steel and plastic water bowls can harbor odors that may turn off some dogs with their keen senses of smell. If seeing your dog drinking from the toilet is a turnoff for you, just keep the lid down and make sure he always has plenty of fresh water in a glass or ceramic bowl available in another room.

A DOG'S HOUSE IS HIS CASTLE

....

Although your dog should spend most of his days and all of his nights inside with you, every dog deserves his very own canine condo. A doghouse will keep him warm and dry and will provide necessary shade on warmer days, especially if he can safely and comfortably stay outside while you are at work or away from home for a few hours.

Doghouses best suit canines who are comfortable hanging out by themselves without becoming overly anxious or indulging in obnoxious nonstop barking.

When creating or selecting a doghouse, factor in these pooch amenities:

- Size the doghouse so that your dog can comfortably turn around and stretch out.

- Make sure the floor is at least 4 inches off the ground and well insulated.

- Give the doghouse four wheels so that you can easily relocate it.

- Build a slanted roof so that snow and rain won't collect on top.

- Select a design with a hinged roof that you can lift for easy cleaning access.

- Make sure the house is amply ventilated, with the entrance facing away from prevailing winds.

- Fasten a thick, clear plastic flap on the entrance to keep out flying insects, rain, sleet, and snow.

- Use only nontoxic paint; dogs are prone to chewing.

- Strew straw or, if the dog isn't allergic, cedar shavings on the floor. Don't use newspapers (the ink can discolor fur and cause allergic reactions) or hay (it tends to get moldy and can cause a fungal infection).

- Keep the doghouse clean and odor free by sweeping it out at least weekly.

FIT *for a* PRINCE

. . . .

Go first-class and turn an ordinary doghouse into
a heated and air-conditioned haven by connecting
it to your own house's heater and air conditioner.
(You'll need to monitor the temperature closely.)

Antifreeze has a sweet flavor that attracts pets, but even a small amount can be deadly if ingested. Take the following steps to prevent an accident:

- Keep your dogs indoors when you are changing or adding antifreeze.

- Look for brands that contain propylene glycol, which is less toxic than ethylene glycol.

- Wipe up any automotive spills immediately and sprinkle sand or kitty litter on the spot.

- Take used antifreeze to a recycling center for proper disposal.

- Make sure that your car has no coolant leaks.

BOREDOM BUSTERS

....

When you're away from home, your dog can't fight boredom or anxiety by working a crossword puzzle, taking up cross-stitching, or writing the Great American Novel. Dogs think and act differently from people. Try keeping the television or radio on low volume as a distraction.

A hollow rubber toy filled with treats should keep your dog mentally and physically busy. Stuff the toy with peanut butter, cream cheese, or kibble. Synthetic hollow bones work well for this, too. Toss them in the dishwasher to clean.

TERRIFIC TIP

Keep baby wipes (unscented, please!) on hand for when your dog has rolled in something smelly but doesn't need an all-out bath. They are also useful for cleaning up minor accidents, especially vomit. Pet supply stores carry dog-specific brands of moist towelettes, ranging from individual travel packs to economy-size tubs.

LOW-STRESS PARTINGS

....

Does your dog wrap his front paws around your calf when you leave the house? Or body slam you in his excitement upon your return? Sadly, we're usually to blame for why some dogs make such a fuss to bid us bye-bye or hug us hello. We're flattered by the shower of attention and we respond in kind. Our response actually exacerbates anxiety and reinforces rowdiness. You can reduce stressful or overly excited partings and greetings by following this advice:

- Don't make a big deal about exiting or entering the house. Stage dress rehearsals. Spend 5 minutes sitting in a chair with your dog by your side. Don't talk to her or touch her; she needs to be in a calm state. Then walk outside for a minute or so. Reenter the house and again ignore your dog, even if she is jumping all over you. Wait a few minutes before greeting her casually. Gradually build up to 10 to 15 minutes between leaving and returning.

- To break your dog's habit of leaping on you when you come in, ignore her for a few minutes before greeting her. Reach for a toy stashed in a basket by the door and toss it to her as soon you step inside. Your dog will learn to unleash her energy on the toy instead of you.

- Confine your pet to a single dog-proofed room or a crate. Dogs feel more secure in smaller spaces.

- Give your dog a job while you're gone by providing him with a treat-dispensing toy. By working for his food, your dog is engaged in scavenging and hunting activities and is less likely to tear up your couch out of boredom or nervousness.

- Leave a recently worn T-shirt in your dog's bed to ease her anxiety.

- Invite trusted neighbors or friends to stop by and play with your dog while you are out.

GOOD TOYS, BAD TOYS

....

When it comes to pet toys, use the same precaution you use with small children: Keep toys with small or removable parts away from your dog. Squeaky toys or stuffed animals with plastic eyes, ribbons, and floppy ears or other loose parts can pose choking hazards for a dog who treats his toys with too much toothy attention.

Dog toys should be fun, interactive, and brightly colored. Choose toys made of strong, safe materials. Topping the list are vinyl, latex, nylon, and simulated lambskin. Select sturdy toys that can pass the chew test. Toys made of hard rubber or nylon are better than soft foam balls that can be easily shredded.

Don't offer an old shoe as a toy. It will teach your puppy or dog that it's okay to chew on all shoes.

Use durable balls that bounce well. Nothing ends a game of fetch faster than a cheap tennis ball that "goes flat" with a single chomp.

There are numerous types and qualities of rawhide chews and bones available. Left lying around to "marinate" (especially out in the yard), these chews run the risk of becoming contaminated with salmonella, which can infect your dog. Each day, pick up your dog's rawhide and rinse it in very hot water to rid it of any germs before giving it back to your dog. Supervise your dog's time with rawhides as they can also pose a choking and obstruction hazard if the dog tries to swallow them.

CELE-BARK *the* HOLIDAYS

....

Dogs don't know the true meaning of Christmas or Hanukkah or Kwanza. They can't fathom why the neighborhood sounds like a battle zone during the Fourth of July, or why strange children wearing even stranger outfits are ringing the doorbell on Halloween and begging for — and receiving! — treats.

Holidays can be anxiety-filled times for our cherished canines. The best way to pamper your dog during these times of celebration is to protect him from harm and give him plenty of calm reassurance and TLC.

- Don't force your dog to wear a bow around his neck during the 12 days of Christmas. He might trip or choke on it. A better option is to buy him a new collar in holiday colors.

- Keep your cherished holiday ornaments, statues, and treasures out of the reach of wagging tails and nosy noses.

- The holidays are stressful enough with all of their activities; they are not a good time to adopt a puppy or add a second dog to your household. Wait until you've settled back into your regular routine before heading to the shelter.

- Avoid edible decorations, such as popcorn or candy canes. A dog acting naughty rather than nice can suffer a stomach upset (not to mention causing a decorated tree upset).

- Don't let your dog gorge on rich holiday leftovers. Instead, indulge him with gourmet canine treats or opt for small bits of lean meat and cooked vegetables without sauces.

- Fill your dog's stocking with dog biscuits and chew toys or a brand new tennis ball.

- Use nontoxic artificial snow and preservative in the water for the Christmas tree.

- Keep your anxious dog in a quiet part of the house during holiday parties.

HAVE *a* HOUND-Y HOLIDAY

....

Your dog may not be as thrilled about human holidays as you are. Instead of always expecting her to take part in your traditions, start a new tradition that you can enjoy together. Celebrate your dog's birthday by inviting over a few of her favorite four-legged friends. Serve some homemade dog biscuits, play games, or have the dogs show off their best tricks.

Keeping Your Chowhound Happy

HAPPY DOG
HAPPY YO[...]

Chapter Four

C HOWTIME RANKS AS THE NUMBER ONE FAVORITE ACTIVITY FOR MOST CANINES. FOR proof, just take a look at your dog when you pick up the empty food bowl. In anticipation, your dog will exhibit the telltale signs that say, "Feed me" — smacking lips, drooling mouth, begging paws, and wiggling body. The way to your dog's heart is definitely directly through his belly, but plan your canine cuisine with your dog's health foremost in mind.

We all like to indulge our doggy pals with their favorite foods and to share our meals with them, but we're slowly killing them with kindness. In fact, one of every three adult dogs can be labeled real chowhounds because they are overweight. Show true love by not overfeeding your dog. Each extra ounce of body fat reduces your dog's longevity, mobility, and vitality.

Is your dog too chubby? Not sure? Here's how to determine if your dog is fit or fat. Standing behind your dog, place both thumbs on his backbone. Run your fingers lightly along his rib cage. If you can't feel the bones through the fur, he's probably overweight.

TERRIFIC TIP

Encourage your dog to romp and play with her doggy friends to burn some calories. Better yet, double up on the workout by going for a hike or a jog together.

Cultivate healthy eating habits. Sure, you want to feed to please, but don't go overboard. If you truly want to pamper your dog at chowtime, feed him the right amount of the right food. That's easier said than done. When two brown, soulful eyes are aimed your way, it's human nature to heap on the helpings. But resist and your dog will live a longer, healthier, and happier life.

To ensure that mealtime is a happy time for both of you, make your dog *think* he's getting more food. Instead of feeding him one big bowl once a day, divide the same amount of chow into three or four mini-meals. Smaller, frequent meals are easier to digest and help your dog's metabolism to work more efficiently.

Never put your dog on a crash diet. You run the risk of his losing more muscle mass than excess fat. Instead, gradually reduce the amount of chow by 10 percent or so weekly. A dog who is 30 percent overweight should take about six months to reach a healthy weight through reduced portions. Work with your veterinarian on an eating plan that slowly but steadily sheds excess weight.

Help your pudgy pooch lose a few pounds by adding more dietary fiber to her meals. Fiber not only improves digestion but also helps lessen the chance of constipation. Good sources of fiber include a tablespoon of canned pumpkin, a few slices of chopped raw carrot, and a spoonful of cooked oatmeal (hold the sugar).

Sprinkle a teaspoon of kelp powder on your dog's food. Or try mixing a capsule of lecithin (open the capsule first) or a teaspoon of organic apple cider vinegar in his water bowl. All three speed up the metabolism and break down fats.

NO SWEETS *for* YOUR SWEET

....

Many dogs love sweet treats, but resist the temptation to share your chocolate chip cookies. Chocolate contains theobromine, a stimulant related to caffeine that is toxic to dogs and can cause vomiting and diarrhea, or even death. Instead, offer your dog a sweet-but-safe substitute: carob. Or even better, dish out some fresh carrots for him to munch on between meals.

DIET DISASTER

....

Sugar-free candy and gum may be sweet treats to you, but the artificial sweetener xylitol can trigger seizures and liver failure in dogs if eaten in large amounts, and "large amount" is an individual measure. "None" is the safe amount.

THE CANINE CHEF

....

For special occasions or just to show how much you love him, prepare a healthy homemade meal for your dog. Becoming a chef for your dog takes more than slipping on a canine-designed apron and enticing your dog with the words "Let's eat!" To keep your cuisine creations safe and healthy, please heed these tips:

1. Wash your hands in warm, soapy water and rinse well before handling food.

2. Wash all produce to clear away any pesticides, dirt, and bugs.

3. Trim fat from meats and drain excess grease from cooked meats to reduce the risk of your dog developing pancreatitis (painful for him and pricey to treat for you).

4. Keep the recipe simple. Preparing a dish for your dog is meant to be fun and bonding, not difficult and stress-filled.

5. Select fresh, and, if possible, organically grown ingredients.

6. Always cook meat, seafood, poultry, and eggs to reduce the risk of salmonella or other parasitic threat. Don't give your dog cooked bones, though — they can splinter.

7. Store leftovers in airtight containers in the refrigerator where they will stay fresh for several days. Or store the extras in the freezer where they will keep for at least three months.

TLC TEMPTATION

....

This recipe will provide two or three full-size meals for a medium-size dog (20 to 40 pounds) though it should only be served as an occasional treat. You can also use it as a tasty topper for your dog's regular kibble; just be sure to cut back on the amount of kibble.

4 ounces lean ground beef
4 ounces low-fat or fat-free cottage cheese
1 cup grated or cooked carrots
1 cup cooked and chopped green beans

1. Cook the ground beef in a pan. Drain off the fat and allow the meat to cool.

2. Add the remaining ingredients and mix well. Serve as a Sunday treat.

3. Keep leftovers refrigerated for up to a week.

TERRIFIC TIP

If your dog is a pest at the table, feed her in a separate room while you're enjoying your dinner. This prevents begging and allows you both to dine without interruption.

If you plan on baking bread, banish your dog from the kitchen. Never leave uncooked bread dough on the counter to rise where a greedy canine could grab it. If your dog decided to do a little counter surfing and gobbled the dough, it could swell inside his stomach and possibly require surgery to remove.

Serve your dog water on the rocks. Help your dog to stay cool and occupied during warm days by giving him a few ice cubes to chew on. The crunchy cubes are fun to eat and provide essential fluids your dog needs to keep from overheating.

For a particularly appreciated treat, freeze low-sodium, fat-free beef or chicken broth in an ice cube tray. Dole the cubes out once a week or so and make sure they are consumed on easy-to-clean tile or linoleum floors and not on your carpets.

Most dogs are game to gulp down anything dropped on the floor in the kitchen without stopping for a safety sniff. That's why it is important to keep the following foods out of paw's — and mouth's — reach:

- *Onions.* They contain large amounts of sulfur, which can destroy red blood cells and cause severe anemic reactions in dogs.

- *Garlic.* Some dogs eat garlic without any problem, but err on the safe side. In large quantities, garlic can damage red blood cells.

- *Grapes.* Dogs can choke on this fruity treat, and too many can also harm a dog's kidneys and liver and possibly contribute to renal failure.

- *Raisins.* They are not a choking hazard like grapes, but can make your dog very ill.

- *Real bones.* They can splinter and cause intestinal obstructions and internal bleeding. They also harbor parasites, especially if your dog opts to bury them in the backyard and let them "marinate" for a week or so before digging them back up for a snack.

- *Raw meat.* It can carry the threat of bacteria, possibly causing your dog to suffer diarrhea or vomiting, although dogs are far less susceptible to food pathogens than humans are.

- *Sushi.* Raw fish, especially smelt, herring, catfish, and carp, contains an enzyme called thiaminase, which destroys the vitamin thiamine (B_1). Cooking destroys this enzyme, so feeding cooked fish to Fido is fine.

LEAPING LIVER!

....

Here's a recipe that will have your dog drooling with delight:

> 1 pound sliced beef liver (save the juice)
> ¼ cup water
> 1 small box corn muffin mix

1. Preheat the oven to 350°F. Spray an 8½ by 11-inch baking pan with nonstick spray.

2. Grind the liver in a food processor one slice at a time. Add a little water with each slice so that you have a liquid.

3. Thoroughly combine the muffin mix and the liver liquid in a large bowl.

4. Pour the liver mix into the pan.

5. Bake for 20 to 25 minutes, or until the middle springs back at your touch.

6. Cool and cut into small cubes, because organ meat, while good for your dog, is too rich to give in large amounts.

Making this recipe will stink up your kitchen (briefly), but the good news is that you can make a big batch and store it in the freezer for up to three months.

Some human food is fine to share with dogs. On special occasions, serve up these tasty treats: one meatball (minus the sauce and portion-size for your dog), a small piece of cooked hamburger, an ounce of boneless broiled chicken, or a dice-size cube of hard cheese.

Use mealtime to address some minor medical conditions. For example, you can give doggy dandruff the brush-off by adding a teaspoon of corn, safflower, peanut, or sunflower oil to your dog's meal two or three times a week. These oils help to replenish the body's natural oils and reduce dry, itchy skin. Just remember to include these teaspoons in your dog's daily caloric needs — especially if you have a small pup.

Your dog will benefit from food containing these ingredients: vitamin E, beta-carotene, gamma linolenic acid, Omega-3 fatty acids, proteins, fiber, glucosamine, and L-carnitines. These substances help to repair cartilage, rejuvenate dry skin, build muscle tissue, boost the immune system, and aid digestion.

Never assume that a low-fat dog food will be a miracle answer to slimming down your chubby canine. Fat helps to keep your dog's coat and skin healthy and provides energy. Just be sure not to give too much fat; ask your veterinarian for guidelines on picking the right high-quality food that suits your dog's age, breed, activity level, and health.

READ *the* LABEL

....

The largest pet food recall in U.S. history happened in the spring of 2007, when it was discovered that Chinese manufacturers were adding melamine, an industrial chemical used to make plastics, to pet food to falsely "beef up" the protein value of the food. Sadly, far too many dogs became sick and died before monitoring systems were improved.

Do your part on behalf of your dog by choosing quality pet food that lists a real meat protein as the first ingredient. Stay clear of cheap foods, especially ones where the first listed ingredient is "by-product" or wheat or other grain.

Check the expiration date on food labels and never serve food that is past its prime. If your dog refuses to eat his usual food, trust his instincts and replace it.

Go easy on the dairy treats. **Cheese is a great calcium source but too much can cause gas or diarrhea. However, a tablespoon or two of plain unsweetened yogurt once or twice a week is a good addition to your dog's diet. It helps to maintain a healthy bacterial balance in the gut.**

Toss out any canned food or moistened kibble that your dog leaves in the bowl after mealtime. Dry kibble can safely stay in the bowl during the day if you share your home with a nibbler.

TERRIFIC TIP

If your guests try to slip treats to your dog from their dinner plates, diplomatically explain that the house rule is not to feed your dog from the table. Explain that you love your dog and want him to watch his manners and his weight.

Did you know that small dogs burn more calories than do large dogs, ounce for ounce? Were you aware that older, less active dogs need fewer calories and that working dogs burn more calories than their couch-lounging counterparts? Factor in your dog's age, weight, activity level, flavor preferences, and health when selecting commercial dog food.

If your dog is a gobbler, limit him to a 20-minute mealtime, removing his dish after that. If there are any leftovers, you may be feeding too much. Slightly reduce the portion.

For a dog who likes to nibble all day, consider an automatic feeder that dispenses a specific amount of dry food over the course of the day. Sprinkle some special freeze-dried treats in with the dry food so that as your dog munches she occasionally finds an extra-tasty tidbit. She'll feel like she's hit a juicy jackpot!

Don't serve food or water in plastic bowls. A "chew hound" can perforate edges, inviting bacteria to thrive in the punctured plastic (not to mention spilling the contents all over the place and potentially cutting into your dog's gums). Also, some dogs are turned off by the smell of plastic or the taste the water picks up. Serve food and water in sturdy ceramic or glass bowls instead.

When introducing a new brand of dog food, make the switch slowly. Otherwise, your dog may experience diarrhea or other digestive upsets. Start with just a small amount of the new food mixed into your dog's current food. Increase that portion gradually while reducing the portion of current food over 10 to 14 days. This time span allows your dog's digestive system to adjust to the new food.

TERRIFIC TIP

Take the guesswork out of food
portions. Use a measuring cup when
doling out dry food, and level off
each scoop. This provides you with
a baseline. If your dog gains weight,
you know to trim back on the size
of each serving.

Set aside time after dinner to walk your dog for at least 20 minutes. Both of you will benefit from an evening stroll. Exercising after a meal raises the metabolism and burns more calories than does sitting on the sofa or in front of the computer after supper. If your dog is a bloat-susceptible breed, take your exercise at an unhurried pace.

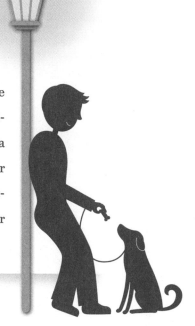

Weigh your dog once a month using the same scale each time. Record the weight to the exact ounce on a notepad near her food containers. A weight gain of a pound on a medium-size adult dog (who weighs between 25 and 45 pounds) over a month's time is your signal to cut back on the chow and step up the exercise time. Two extra pounds on a medium-size dog is like 10 to 20 pounds on a person.

Some dogs are always "starving." Fool your hungry hound into thinking he is getting a heap more chow by adding steamed vegetables to his meal. Vegetables are low in calories but have plenty of fiber, which helps satisfy your dog's appetite so that he leaves his bowl feeling full, not fat.

Keep these foods on hand to add a homemade touch to commercial kibble:

- lean ground beef or turkey
- cooked beef liver
- brown rice
- bran
- corn oil
- low-fat or salted cottage cheese
- carrots
- scrambled eggs
- cooked, chopped cauliflower and potatoes

TERRIFIC TIP

Just as you do for yourself, opt to boil, broil, bake, or steam meats and fish for your dogs. Never give them fried foods. Also avoid cooking with lard or coconut oil because both are loaded with saturated fats.

MARVELOUS MUTT MEATBALLS

....

This is, paws down, the favorite homemade recipe for my dogs, Chipper and Cleo. I hope your canine chums chow down with delight, too!

> ½ pound ground beef or turkey
> ½ cup grated cheddar cheese
> 1 carrot, finely chopped
> ½ cup breadcrumbs
> 1 egg, whisked
> 3 tablespoons tomato paste (low-sodium)

1. Preheat the oven to 350°F.

2. Combine all the ingredients in a medium-size mixing bowl.

3. Scoop out by the spoonful and roll into mini-size meatballs.

4. Place the meatballs on a cookie sheet sprayed with nonfat cooking spray.

5. Bake for 15 to 20 minutes.

6. Cool, then store in the refrigerator in a container with a lid for a week or in the freezer for one to two months.

Although most dog foods are fortified, dogs don't always get the right amount of the vitamins and minerals they need. Make your dog her healthiest with supplements. Before you start, though, discuss the proper supplement dosages with a holistic veterinarian. You can locate one in your area by contacting the American Holistic Veterinary Medical Association at *www.ahvma.org*.

GIVING SUPPLEMENTS

....

Pamper your dog's health by following these supplement guidelines:

- Take into account your dog's size, age, physical condition, and stress level.

- Always follow label directions and never over-supplement.

- Introduce one supplement at a time to your dog's breakfast or dinner. Wait a few days to see if there are any side effects before adding another supplement.

- Don't use more than one multi-type supplement; it can lead to doubling up.

DOGGONE GOODNESS

....

Treat your dog to an occasional home-cooked meal that is healthy and delicious. Surprise him on his birthday, for finishing dog obedience training, or for learning a new trick. Here's a favorite recipe that my grandma taught me to make for Crackers, our beagle.

1 cup raw rolled oats

3 whisked eggs, baked in the oven for 10 minutes at 350°F

½ cup cottage cheese (small curd)

1 cup raw carrots (diced or grated)

½ cup cooked, chopped or ground turkey, drained

Brewer's yeast (optional)

1. Bring 2 cups of water to a boil on the stovetop. Add the oats, cover, reduce to medium heat, and cook for 3 minutes.

2. Turn off the heat and let the pan with water and oats stand for another 10 minutes; add the rest of the ingredients.

3. Spoon the mixture into your dog's bowl. As an added treat, sprinkle some brewer's yeast on top.

Store leftovers in the refrigerator for up to a week.

Think a dog bowl is just a bowl? Think again. Engineers have created special water bowls designed to stop spillage and to prevent dogs from gulping too quickly. They've also designed food bowls with elevated centers to make dogs work more for their chow, reducing the tendency to wolf down food and develop indigestion, or even bloat, a condition that tends to affect large deep-chested dogs.

Once a week, put your dog's food and water bowls into the dishwasher or wash them well with soap and warm water for a thorough cleaning to prevent the growth of bacteria such as *E. coli* or salmonella.

THE GRASS IS ALWAYS GREENER

....

Ever wonder why your dog chews grass? Does he like the taste? Maybe. Maybe not. Dogs most likely ingest grass because it provides some of the roughage and nutrients they need. Dogs also seem to know instinctively that a few bites of grass can help overcome a bout of indigestion. So it's fine to let your canine "cow" graze away, but make sure he sticks to chemical-free turf.

Hands-on Health
(*The Owner's Manual*)

Chapter
Five

HAPPY DOG
HAPPY YOU

....

LET'S SEE A SHOW OF PAWS — HOW MANY DOGS JUST DROOL WITH DELIGHT AT THE CHANCE TO see the veterinarian? Hmmm . . . not many. It's not a trip that many people relish, either. But just like us, dogs need to receive complete checkups at least once a year. In addition to providing a secure home, a healthy diet, and plenty of exercise for your canine chum, you are the front line of defense for bringing out his healthy best. That means shielding him from disease and protecting him from injury.

....

Treat your dog like a toddler. Both are naturally curious and need your guidance to keep them out of harm's way. Employ these simple tactics:

- Install childproof latches on cabinets within nose and paw reach.

- Cover cords with chew-resistant coverings.

- Keep liquid potpourris and lit candles out of reach of your dog's wagging tail or face.

- Keep small items like sewing needles and pennies away from your curious canine.

TERRIFIC TIP

Show how much you love your
dog by enrolling in a pet first-aid
class. Contact your local humane
society or the American Society for
the Prevention of Cruelty to Animals
(ASPCA) to learn about classes
in your area.

CRITICAL INFO

. . . .

Post this number in a highly visible place, such as on your refrigerator door:

24-hour ASPCA Animal Poison Control Center
1-888-426-4435
Web site: *www.aspca.org*

Please note there is a consultation fee that can be applied to your credit card, but it is worth the price if you can save your pet's life.

Signs of poisoning include listlessness, abdominal pain, vomiting, diarrhea, muscle tremors, lack of coordination, and fever. When you call, provide the symptoms your pet is displaying as well as the name and amount of the poison she was exposed to and when the exposure occurred. The breed, age, sex, and weight of your pet are also important.

Assemble a first-aid kit for your dog. A well-stocked kit should contain:

- Cold packs

- Nonstick sterile gauze pads

- Lightweight adhesive tape that won't stick to wounds

- Cotton balls

- Cotton-tipped ear swabs

- Antiseptic wipes

- Surgical scissors

- Tweezers

- Antibiotic ointment

- Hydrogen peroxide

- Styptic powder to stop minor bleeding

- Clean white cotton sock to wrap an injured paw or limb

- Diphenhydramine (Benadryl) for bites and stings

- Coated buffered aspirin

- Activated charcoal

WORD of WARNING

....

Never give acetaminophen or ibuprofen to your dog. These over-the-counter medications can cause ulcers and can be toxic.

Keep poisonous houseplants safely out of your dog's reach by hanging them on ceiling hooks. Scout around the yard, too; if your dog helps himself to pickings from your flower boxes, yard, and garden as if they were his personal salad bar, be sure there aren't poisonous plants among the choices. Dogs can become ill or even die after ingesting azalea, daffodil bulbs, dieffenbachia, geranium, holly, impatiens, ivy, mistletoe, morning glory, oleander, philodendron, and poinsettia. For a complete list, check the Web site of the Humane Society of the United States at *www.hsus.org*.

KEEP THOSE CANINES
(*Teeth*) CLEAN!

....

Check your dog's mouth regularly for signs of deterioration. If you note bleeding gums, pale gums, persistent foul breath, tartar buildup, decay, sores, or broken or missing teeth, make an appointment with your veterinarian.

Don't dismiss doggy breath. An unpleasant odor could be an early warning sign of gingivitis or other dental problems. In fact, 80 percent of dogs lacking dental care develop gum and teeth problems by age three, according to the American Veterinary Dental Society.

Check with your vet about possible reduced rates for teeth cleaning and oral surgery in February, which is National Pet Dental Health Month.

Provide fresh water daily. Because dogs slobber saliva when they slurp, bacteria can build up inside bowls containing water that is more than two days old.

TERRIFIC TIP

Help your dog chase away surface tartar by giving him dental chew products, raw carrots, and hard biscuits to chew on. There are many good canine dental care products, so keep experimenting until you find a couple that your dog enjoys.

To get your dog used to the tooth-brushing routine, break it down into a few steps done over a series of brushing sessions. Dip your finger into beef bouillon before rubbing it gently over her mouth and teeth. When she accepts this routine, add gauze over your finger and gently scrub the teeth in a circular motion. Finally, introduce a soft toothbrush designed for dogs and use meat-flavored toothpaste.

TAKE *a* HIKE

....

Dogs who are regularly walked a minimum of 20 minutes a day since puppyhood are less likely to develop age-related disorders or digestive problems.

TIME *for a* PET-ICURE

....

Long nails are definitely not in fashion in the dog world. Clipping your dog's nails can be easy and quick with the right approach and tools. Treat your dog to regular pedicures to avoid snags in the carpet, infections, or injuries. Here are some tips for turning a routine chore into some quality time together:

- Begin stress-free manicures when your dog is still a puppy.

- Handle her in a quiet, confined place to eliminate any distractions — or escape routes.

- Touch, tickle, and massage your dog's feet regularly. This gets her used to having her paws handled and reduces her anxiety when you clip her nails.

- Speak in a calm, reassuring tone during the process.

- Cut one or two nails the first time, and gradually, as your dog learns to accept the clipping without fussing, work your way to all four feet.

- Use clippers that are specifically designed for dogs. They do the job better and are safer than human nail clippers.

- Clip your dog's nails after a bath or a swim, when the nails are softer.

- If your dog has clear nails, trim just above the "quick" area. That's the pinkish part of the nail where the blood vessels are. If your dog has dark nails, just nip off the tip every two weeks.

- Keep a styptic pencil or styptic powder within reach in case you accidentally cut too deeply and cause bleeding. If you're temporarily out, sprinkle cornstarch on the injured toe to stop the bleeding.

- Always finish with praise and a treat.

With the exception of a few breeds, dogs shed a lot. Brushing your dog's fur promotes a healthy coat because it removes loose hair and stimulates blood flow to the skin. Regular brushing will leave your dog's coat shining and keep your home from turning into a giant ball of fur.

GO *with the* FLOW

....

Always brush in the direction of fur growth. Going against the grain can irritate the skin and make your dog want to flee the scene when you pull out the grooming supplies. Use straight strokes for longhaired breeds; circular motions can break hair and cause tangles.

And make sure you have the right tools for your dog's type of hair: Double-coated breeds such as huskies and corgis fare best with comb-type tools while curly coated breeds like poodles do better with wide-toothed slicker brushes.

TERRIFIC TIP

Loosen a shedding coat with a blow dryer. Turn it to a low, cool setting to avoid burning the skin and brush gently to remove loose fur.

S-T-R-E-T-C-H IT OUT

....

Dogs know instinctively how to stretch properly and loosen up their muscles. Notice that they stretch when they first awaken and that they indulge in tail-to-nose stretches several times during the day. Stretching reduces muscle tension and stiffness and improves circulation of blood and lymph. It enhances flexibility and range of motion, which reduces the chance of injury. Join your dog for a little canine yoga every morning and your muscles will feel better, too.

Become your dog's personal massage therapist. By applying the right therapeutic touch to your dog, you deliver health benefits and strengthen your emotional bond. Follow these tips for a soothing session:

- Approach your dog slowly and speak soothingly.

- Choose a time when you both feel calm and relaxed.

- Wash your hands to rinse off creams and lotions.

- Pay attention to your dog's feedback. If he lies still, gives you a sleepy glance, or dozes off, you've got the right touch. If he wiggles, resists, or tries to escape, end the session.

- Stroke the muscles toward the heart to enhance healthy blood flow.

- Apply steady strokes without pressing too deeply.

- Enroll in a canine massage class. Look for a licensed massage therapist with certification in dog massage.

TERRIFIC TIP

Toss a blanket into the dryer for 10 to 15 minutes and drape it over your dog on chilly nights. The dry heat eases joint aches and increases flexibility, and the coziness will help her to sleep more soundly.

SPLISH, SPLASH, DOGGY'S TAKING *a* BATH

....

How often you bathe your dog depends on the climate and the degree of doggy odor emitted. Some dogs need regular bathing, while others can escape with a yearly scrubbing. Few dogs sit at the bathroom door with a towel draped around their necks, tail tapping impatiently in anticipation of a bath; however, you hold the key to making baths a splashing good time.

- Size up your dog. For dogs less than 15 pounds, kitchen sinks make ideal tubs because they are at the right height for you and may offer a spray attachment. Utility sinks or bathtubs work best for medium-size dogs. Large breeds fare best in shower stalls or commercial dog washes.

- Expect to get wet. Wear old clothes and a rubberized apron in anticipation of those full-body shakes. You might even don your bathing suit!

- Place a towel in the sink or tub to keep your dog from slipping. Put other towels and cleaning supplies within easy reach.

- Put cotton balls in your dog's ears to keep water from entering his ear canals.

- Fill a large jug with warm water and add two drops of shampoo. Pour the jug of soapy water over the dog's coat before you begin wetting her down. This permits water to more quickly penetrate your dog's natural oil coating. Then work the shampoo evenly into her coat with your fingertips, not your nails.

- Once you've rinsed off the soap, swathe her in two towels. Let those two towels soak up most of the water. Then close the curtain or shower stall door and let her shake. Finish with a third dry towel.

- Speak to your dog in calm, upbeat, reassuring tones from start to finish. Let her know what you're planning to do each step of the way. She may not understand your words, but your meaning will come across loud and clear.

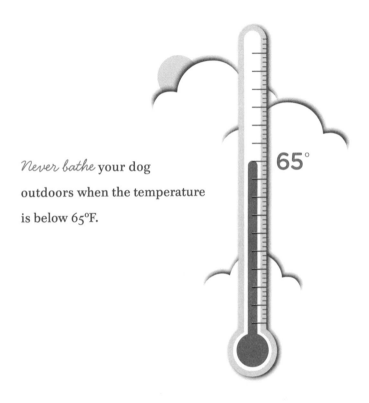

Never bathe your dog outdoors when the temperature is below 65°F.

65°

When you bathe your dog, distract her by singing songs or playing music in the bathroom. You can also provide a dog-pleasing distraction by putting a tablespoon of peanut butter on the wall facing your dog so she can lick it off while she's being washed.

Bath time is a great time to reinforce good behavior — reward your dog for sitting or standing patiently with small bits of a very special treat doled out over the course of the procedure. When it's all over, don't let her run off and hide (or worse yet, roll in the mud) — take her for a walk or have a good romp in the yard.

Treat your dog to a do-it-yourself dog-washing emporium. I can wash Cleo in the sink in my garage, but at 60 pounds, Chipper won't fit, and I don't want her golden retriever-husky hair clogging up my shower drain. So when the need arises, we head to Dippy Dog Wash, a place that offers waist-high, step-up tubs, plenty of towels, and all the bathing supplies necessary to let Chipper sport a clean, groomed coat.

TERRIFIC TIP

When you can't bathe your stinky dog, sprinkle some baking soda on his coat. Use your fingers to work it into the fur. Baking soda is a natural deodorizer, and it won't harm your dog.

Let sleeping dogs lie and dream undisturbed. Yes, dogs definitely dream. Research shows that small dogs dream more frequently than do large dogs, but large dogs enjoy longer dreams. What they dream about remains a coveted canine secret, but my money is on raiding the kitchen trash can, chasing the neighbor's cat, and going for car rides.

If you need to awaken your dog, for safety's sake, do so gently. Tap on the floor, clap your hands, or softly call his name instead of touching him. This allows his subconscious to register your presence without startling him too abruptly. Let your dog stand up, stretch, and jump down from the bed or chair on his own.

Bubble gum and dogs don't mix — especially if your unlucky dog gets a wad of gum stuck to his paws or fur. Remove it painlessly and quickly with peanut butter mixed with vegetable oil. Dab this mixture on the area and rub gently to loosen and remove the gum.

A backup option: Apply *Goo Gone*, a product found in supermarkets and hardware stores. Rinse completely after the gum is gone.

On or around your dog's seventh birthday, give the best present that can't be wrapped in a gift box: a comprehensive vet checkup that includes blood and urine testing. The lab results will provide a baseline of your dog's condition and help your veterinarian to customize her care.

Show your golden oldie how grateful you are for her being your furry friend for so many years by booking wellness exams at least twice a year with your veterinarian. Dogs age five to seven times faster than people do, so an annual visit for a seven-year-old dog is equivalent to a person visiting a family physician once every six years or so.

Treat your aging dog like a VIP — a Very Important Pooch. The graying of his muzzle and the slowing of his step should be signals to increase your pampering. Your dog has been loyal to you since puppyhood. Now it's time to show him some extra appreciation. Here are a few easy ways to pamper your senior citizen:

- Place water bowls in different locations inside the house. Older dogs tend to drink less. With water readily available, your dog is less likely to become dehydrated.

- Add a chewable pet vitamin recommended by your vet to your dog's daily diet. These vitamins provide many important nutrients your aging dog needs.

- Continue daily exercise, but make sure that it's the right kind. A brisk walk might be better suited to your aging pal even if he's always gone on long runs with you.

- As your dog's hearing and vision fade, keep him on a leash during walks, especially at night. You need to hone your senses to keep him out of harm's way.

- Keep your dog's sleeping area warm and cozy.

- Apply a warm water bottle or heated towel over arthritic joints. Massage stiff spots with gentle circular motions.

- Install ramps to help your dog climb up stairs, into the car, or up onto the bed. There are many models available, but the best ones are wide enough to be secure and feature nonslip surfaces for greater traction.

DO-IT-YOURSELF DOG RAMP

....

You can make your own ramp for an aging or arthritic dog from a lightweight but sturdy foam-core board, available at art supply stores. Make sure the board is thick enough and wide enough for your dog to walk on safely. Have it cut long enough to provide a gradual slope, not a steep slant. Cover it with nonskid rubber carpet padding for gripping power.

For your arthritic dog, provide glucosamine-chondroitin capsules to improve mobility. This supplement stimulates production of synovial fluid, the body's natural joint lubricant. Ask your vet for more information.

Show true compassion for all dogs by having your dog spayed or neutered before six months of age. Need a reason? Here are some good ones:

- Female dogs spayed before their first heat are 99.9 percent less likely to develop reproductive cancer.

- Neutered males have fewer prostate problems and are less likely to roam, fight, or urine mark in the house.

- One female dog and her offspring can produce 67,000 dogs in just six years.

- Only one in four dogs finds a permanent, loving home.

- More than eight million dogs and cats are destroyed in this country each year because there are not enough homes for them.

A SPOONFUL *of* SUGAR?

....

Many dogs detest taking pills, but there are ways to make the medicine go down with little or no fuss. The quickest method is to insert the pill into a ball of moist dog food or a small lump of cheese and toss it to your dog as a treat. Most dogs will gulp it down without a thought. Follow with a dog biscuit or another treat to make sure the pill was swallowed.

If your dog is on to you and keeps spitting out the pill, try plan B: Open his jaws wide and pop the pill on top of his tongue as far back as possible. Then hold his jaws closed and massage his throat. Try blowing a quick puff of air into his face. When he blinks, he automatically swallows. Then give him a treat to make up for blowing in his face!

OPEN WIDE

....

To persuade your dog to open up for a pill, place the palm of your hand over the top of his nose and gently press your fingers against the skin along his upper teeth on one side of his mouth and your thumb against the other side. Slight upward pressure at the same time will usually encourage your dog to open his mouth. The feel of his own skin against his teeth discourages him from biting down on the tips of your fingers. This also keeps your hand away from the front of his mouth where he might snap at you.

TERRIFIC TIP

If your dog is in dire need of
professional grooming but is terrified
of the car, hire a mobile groomer to
come to your home. Most arrive in
vans with stainless steel tubs with hot
and cold water, hydraulic grooming
tables, high-velocity dryers, and
vacuum systems.

VITAL SIGNS

....

Learn how to check your dog's TPR (temperature, pulse, and respiration). It's easy to do and strengthens your bond through touch. If you know what your dog's normal vital signs are, you'll be better equipped to recognize when he is sick or overstressed.

Temperature: A canine temperature is taken rectally, which should be no big deal, but you may need help restraining your dog at first if he won't stay still. A digital thermometer makes your job quicker and easier, not to mention more accurate. Normal temperature is 100.5–102.5°F.

Pulse: **A normal resting heart rate for a small dog ranges between 140 and 160 beats per minute; for a medium dog, between 120 and 140; and for a large dog, between 60 and 80. To check, position your dog on his side and slide your hand to the crease where the top of the rear leg meets the body. Feel for the groove where an artery is located and press lightly with your index and middle fingers. Count the pulse for a minute. Or measure a 20-second pulse and multiply by 3.**

Respiration: **Observe your dog when he is resting and breathing normally. An adult dog typically takes between 15 and 30 breaths per minute.**

Give your dog baby food during mild bouts of diarrhea. Dogs really go for poultry and lamb. Stick with meat flavors — vegetables can make the diarrhea worse. Mix it with overcooked white rice. A small dog can eat one jar a day; a medium dog, two; and a large dog, three. If diarrhea persists for more than three days, though, or is watery or bloody, check with your vet, as your dog is at risk for dehydration.

Take the fright out of vet visits. If you've just moved or your veterinarian has relocated, a trip to the new office can be just as scary for you as it is for your dog. Word of mouth is a terrific way to locate a compassionate and skillful veterinarian. Talk with pet-owning neighbors, friends, and coworkers for recommendations.

Ask to tour a new veterinary clinic before booking your first appointment. High-quality clinics will gladly guide you through their facilities and answer your questions. Look for cleanliness in the waiting room, exam rooms, labs, and kennel areas. Find out whether the clinic has evening and weekend hours and if it accommodates after-hours emergencies. Ask about continuing education classes for staff as well as specialties they may have.

Treat your dog to a practice run when introducing her to a new dog doc. Bring your dog into the clinic and let her investigate. Have the vet and his staff give healthy treats to your dog so that she associates the clinic and staff with good thoughts. Then schedule an appointment for an official physical exam. And don't forget to pack the treats!

Bark in the Park: *Life with a Party Animal*

HAPPY DOG
HAPPY YO

Chapter
Six

CHAPTER 6

THERE'S NO QUESTION THAT DOGS ARE BORN PARTY ANIMALS. THEY ARE NOTHING LIKE CATS, who prefer a party of one. Dogs are social critters who like to have fun — both with two-leggers and four-leggers (and the occasional tripod), so it's important to get your dog out of the house. Outings strengthen doggy manners, increase canine confidence, and amuse you and your pal. Your dog is always up for wherever you plan to go and whatever you plan to do, so latch on to that happy mood and unleash your inner pooch!

TAKE *a* WALK *on the* WAG SIDE

....

I've never liked the word "*diet.*" The first three letters sound so un-fun. Let's boycott that word! There's a more fulfilling way to stay in shape that starts with the same letter: d-o-g. Starting immediately, recruit your dog as your workout buddy and the two of you can achieve fitness and maintain good health while you have some fun along the way.

Most dogs happily live by the motto, "Have leash, will travel." When you grab the leash, it's hard not to break into a grin as your dog dashes to the door and does an impromptu dance. Hey, the great outdoors beckons! And guess what? People who walk with dogs walk an average of eight times as far each week as people who are pet-less on their outings. This just proves that dogs are good for our hearts in so many ways.

TERRIFIC TIP

The more fun commands you give
your dog on a walk, the more she will
focus on you rather than oncoming
dogs and scurrying squirrels.
Purposeful play reinforces your
control over your dog and increases
her respect for you as a cool leader.

CHANGE *of* PACE

....

On your walks around the block, surprise your dog by slowing down your gait and saying, "s-l-o-w" in a stretched-out voice. See if he'll move like a furry turtle. Then pick up the pace to a near run while encouraging him to go "Fast, fast, fast!"

Each time your dog complies, reward him with a small food treat or praise. Trust me, your dog will start paying more attention to you in anticipation of your change of pace.

Control your dog, especially on busy sidewalks, by using a six-foot or four-foot nylon or leather leash. I'm not a fan of those plastic-handled leashes with the zip lines that allow dogs to dash 10 feet or more in front of you. Before you have time to retract the line, your dog could run into the street, mix it up with an unfriendly dog, or knock over a child. Bigger dogs can break the line or yank the handle out of your hand and escape.

With such a long leash, you unintentionally surrender control of the walk to your dog who may be so far out in front of you that you can't get his attention quickly to keep him out of harm's way. On walks, you should be calling the shots — and the turns and stops — not your dog.

GOING *to the* DOGS

....

Staging regular playtime sessions and allowing yourself to act goofy may produce better behavior in your dog. Animal behaviorists report that stepping out of an I-give-the-orders-in-this-house role actually strengthens your connection with your dog.

If your dog has no dominant tendencies, try initiating a play session with your dog by acting like a crazy canine. Go down on all fours, raise your rear end in the air, and stretch your arms on the floor to mimic the universal canine cue for fun: the play bow. Give your dog a friendly high-pitched yip, shake your booty, and offer a few playful sideways glances his way. Once he overcomes his amazement, he'll be delighted to romp with you.

GES-HOUND-*HEIT!*

....

Don't underestimate the power of a sneeze, especially in a little dog. During play, many dogs, particularly small breeds, become so excited that they start to sneeze. Behavior experts agree there is nothing but fun attached to this form of *ah-choo*, but they cannot explain why this physical response occurs during moments of glee.

Reduce the risk of a snarling, tense, dog-meet-dog encounter during a walk by speaking in a friendly, upbeat tone and instructing your dog to "watch me" or "walk nicely" as a distraction as you approach an oncoming canine. Your happy voice is a calming signal to your dog, and your verbal cues convey that you are in control. Speaking sternly and tightening the leash conveys the message, especially to a dominant dog, that you are feeling uneasy about the encounter and that he should shift into serious-dog mode and possibly step in to protect you.

Once you are certain of your dog's recall (meaning she reliably comes when you call her and won't go tearing off into the sunset after a squirrel), let her enjoy unleashed freedom in safe areas. You can fence in your backyard, visit a dog park or a dog-welcoming beach, or find a great hiking trail where she can romp and run.

Enjoy the sight of those flapping ears and that tongue-hanging-out grin. Don't let her roam out of sight though; periodically call her back to you to make sure that she doesn't forget her manners.

TERRIFIC TIP

If you call your dog over to you and then let her go run free again, she'll learn that returning to you doesn't always mean that playtime is over.

Treat your dog to an aerobic workout by encouraging him to sprint back and forth in your backyard or other safe confined area. Every morning Chipper, my golden retriever-husky, speeds back and forth in the yard as I shout out, "Go, devil dog, go!"

If you're so inspired, join your dog in his sprints. During inclement weather, hallway sprints can be a suitable substitute, depending on the size of your dog — and your hallway.

Play hide-and-seek with your dog when you are out on walks and your dog is safely running off leash. When he's distracted by a yummy scent, slip behind a tree or duck behind a big rock. Call his name and reward him for finding you. Or just wait a few minutes and see how long it takes him to notice your absence — most dogs don't like having their owners out of sight. This fun game is a great way to reinforce the "come" cue and teach your dog to pay attention to your whereabouts.

CANINE CLIMATE CONTROL

....

You may not be able to bring Mother Nature to heel, but you can buffer your pooch from extreme temperatures. Protection is especially important for very young and very old dogs.

When the weather outside is frightful, keep your dog warm and help him to dodge hypothermia with these helpful hints:

- Use a doggy rain slicker (with hood) to shelter your dog during soggy potty breaks.

- Time your dog's outdoor exposure on the basis of the thickness of her winter coat, her age, and her weight.

- Wash your dog's paws after exposure to the chemical salts used to melt ice. They can irritate footpads and may be toxic if the dog licks her paws.

- If your dog will tolerate them, use booties to protect her toes from harsh conditions. Or try a layer of paw-protecting wax, available from pet supply stores and catalogs.

Dogs pant through their mouths and sweat from their footpads to reduce body temperature, a far less efficient system than the human method of perspiring through thousands of pores. During the dog days of summer when the sun is bright and humidity seems to drip from trees, keep your dog cool by following these tips:

- Take your walks in the early morning or late evening when temperatures are lower.

- If you must walk in the middle of the day, stick to grassy areas and stay away from searing asphalt.

- Dab a little sunscreen around the eyes, ears, nose, and underbellies of light-colored, finely haired dogs.

- Designate a shaded plastic kiddy pool in your yard as your dog's personal water wonderland.

- Recognize that black and dark brown dogs are more prone to heat exhaustion than are white or light-colored dogs. Give them extra shade.

- Go easy on exercise if your dog has a short, pushed-in face. These dogs find it more difficult to breath in hot, humid weather.

COLD-WEATHER WATCH

....

Use common sense when exposing your dog to winter conditions. A healthy adult dog sporting a thick winter coat can tolerate a 20-minute walk in 25°F weather. A senior dog barely tipping the scales at 10 or 15 pounds shouldn't be out for more than 10 minutes when it's that cold. Thin-coated and smaller dogs may need doggy coats when venturing outside if the temperature is 40°F or below. Pay attention to her signals: A shivering dog is a cold dog — bring her inside pronto!

If you don't have kids in your house, bring out your inner teacher and expose your dog to youngsters by showing a dog-loving child how to practice cool tricks with your well-behaved dog. My young friend Weston likes to join Chipper and me on our walks, but he is too small to handle the leash duties. Instead, we take mini-breaks while I give Weston step-by-step instructions on asking Chipper to "sit," "gimme five," and catch tossed treats like an outfielder. Weston beams and his confidence grows. Chipper enjoys the treats and the time spent with Weston. It's a win-win for all!

If you're a bit shy or are looking for ways to meet new people, check out the latest trend: Yappy Hours. These people-pooch mixers may be hosted by animal shelters, pet boutiques, and pet-friendly hotels. Most dogs drink their water straight up, though some prefer ice cubes, while their human companions can order their favorite beverages — hold the water bowl. People feel more comfortable striking up a conversation when there is a dog present. It's a great way to bond with your dog and meet other pet lovers!

ADOPT *a* WALKER

....

If you don't have time to walk your dog as much as you'd like, investigate the possibility of time-sharing your lovable mutt with someone who loves dogs but doesn't live with one. You may have a retired neighbor who would love to take a stroll with a canine companion in the middle of the day or know a kid who could visit after school and even do homework while your dog enjoys having some company.

LET'S PARTY!

. . . .

Turn your backyard into a woofing, wagging wonderland by hosting a celebration for your favorite dogs and their people. The keys to a successful dog party are to have plenty of games and treats and loads of supervision. Set a time limit of no more than two hours. Otherwise you will have to contend with a pack of pooped pups.

Dog parties are terrrr-ific for canines. They bolster that bond between people and pets and increase your "stock value" in your dog's view because you are providing so much fun. Dog parties are good for people, too. They remind us to live in the moment instead of fretting about work, chores, or plans for tomorrow. It's a chance to relax, laugh, and not take yourself too seriously.

TEN GOOD REASONS *to* PARTY *with* YOUR PUP

. . . .

If you're looking for a reason to bring out the party animal in people and dogs, let me offer these celebratory suggestions:

- Adoption anniversary

- Birthday celebration (yours or your dog's)

- Prize-winning pooch (in any sort of competition)

- Puppy or obedience school graduation

- Canine wedding (not legal in any of the 50 states)

- Fund-raiser for local animal shelter (October is Adopt-a-Shelter-Dog month)

- Halloween (or "howl-o-ween" as the hounds say)

- National Dog Day (August 26)

- Get-together for dog park pals

- Just for fun (you don't really *need* a reason)

Your dog will never tell you to limit your singing to the shower, so take advantage of your appreciative audience and sing dog-themed songs such as "Who Let the Dogs Out," "B-I-N-G-O," and "Shake, Dog, Shake." Even better, create your own canine tune that matches your dog's personality. Here's one I wrote for my dogs:

(sung to the tune of "Take Me Out to the Ball Game")

Take me out to the woof park, take me out to the dogs.
Take off my leash and let me fly
So I can play with that Lab nearby.
For it's paws, paws up for the woof park;
If we don't go, it's a shame.
For it's one, two, three woofs we shout
For the fun dog games!

CATERING *to* CANINES

....

Seek out the perfect party location. Some pet-friendly metropolitan areas love to cater indoor canine parties. The Barking Hounds Village Lofts in Atlanta and the Biscuits & Bath Doggy Village in New York City, for example, regularly stage dog parties for a variety of occasions.

In fact, the first doggy wedding at the Big Apple locale featured a mutt named Cinder who wore a veil and a mutt named Max who sported a bow tie at the altar. They exchanged bow-vows that included "we faithfully promise never to bark at or bite each other except in loving play."

LET *the* GAMES BEGIN

....

Here are some fun games that you and your guests can play at a party. (Hint: Invite only dogs who can mind their manners, have no food aggression, and heed basic obedience cues.)

Begging for Biscuits Line up all the dogs in a row in "sit" positions. Have each person hold a tempting treat above their dog's head and slowly raise the treat higher to encourage their dog to balance their weight on their back legs and lift their bodies up. This helps strengthen a dog's back and abdominal muscles and is especially good for large or long-backed dogs.

Test of Wills Ask people to put their dogs in "down" positions. On the count of three, have them place a treat about four inches from their dog's nose and say, "leave it." Owners cannot touch their dogs or pull back on the leashes. The winner is the dog who resists his treat the longest and waits for the okay from his owner. This game is an entertaining way to reinforce the "leave it" command.

Woof Water Relay Give each person-dog pair a small cup and a large cup. Put a large bucket of water at the starting line and line up the large cups at the finish line. Holding the small cup filled with water in the same hand as the leash, each person must walk to the finish line as fast as possible and empty the small cup into the large cup. Then the teams run back to refill their small cups from the bucket. The winner is the first team to fill its large cup. This is a great way to reinforce the habit of walking nicely without pulling.

HAPPY BARK-DAY *to* YOU

....

Here is a naturally sweet, colorful, and flavorful cake that is easy to make.

PEANUT BUTTER CARROT CAKE

....

1 cup flour
1 tsp baking soda
1 cup shredded carrots
½ cup cottage cheese
⅓ cup honey
¼ cup peanut butter
¼ cup vegetable oil
1 egg
1 tsp vanilla

1. Mix flour and baking soda. Add remaining ingredients.

2. Pour into greased 8-inch round cake pan and bake at 350°F for 30 minutes. Let cool.

3. Puree cottage cheese in blender for icing. Decorate with more peanut butter and carrots.

Always supervise when party foods are doled out in order to avoid a fight. When it is time to serve the "pup-cakes," for instance, have everyone leash their dogs and position themselves inside hula hoops placed on the ground or stand at least six feet from the nearest person–dog duo.

Make the best of a new snowfall, especially if you have a dog who thrives in chilly temperatures. Test your dog's tracking talents by hiding a few of his favorite treats in the snowbanks in the backyard. Then take him outside and encourage him to find these tasty treasures. While he is on a seek-and-eat mission, indulge your inner child by making a snow angel. Your dog will probably run to join the fun.

With all of the strict municipal leash laws, you may think it's impossible to find a place to let your dog run unleashed at full stride. Good news: More and more dog parks are springing up around the country. These parks allow dogs to run and play in a safe and inviting environment. Check out the Web site *www.dogpark.com* for a list of dog-friendly places in your area.

If there isn't already a dog park in your community, take the initiative and establish one. Don't forget to enlist the aid of dog-haters. Sounds strange, but these people are likely to support designated public places for pooches to romp off-leash — that way they don't have to encounter dog "deposits" on the local soccer field or worry about loose dogs in people parks.

PROPER PET-IQUETTE

....

Dogs just want to have fun, but certain rules apply to make the dog park a happy — and safe — place for all. Among some common rules are the following:

- Make sure that your dog has up-to-date vaccinations, is healthy, and is wearing identification tags.

- Leave puppies at home until they've had all of their puppy shots and have demonstrated the ability to sit, stay, and come.

- Keep an eye on your dog at all times, and never detach the leash until you've reached the designated off-leash area.

- Bring water along (although most places provide drinking fountains at dog-eye levels, they sometimes go on the fritz), but leave food in your car. This is a playground, not a picnic area. No one wants to start a food fight.

- Bring extra plastic bags, just in case the park doesn't provide them or the supply has run out, so you can scoop your dog's poop promptly.

- Never bring more dogs from your household than you can control. The maximum is three or four, depending on how well behaved they are and how much they stick together.

Pay attention to your dog's body language and watch approaching dogs in case you need to stop a fight before it starts. If you see staring, stiff legs, face-to-face encounters, tense mouths, and flattened ears, try to distract the animals with an activity or a toy to change the mood.

Keep your leash handy to use in case you need to separate feuding dogs. Grab the leash with an end in each hand, loop it in front of your dog's chest, and pull back. Never try to intervene by grabbing a collar — you could easily be bitten.

Another option to break up two dogs is the "wheelbarrow" method. You grab the back legs of your dog while the other person does the same for his dog. One of you stays in that position long enough for the other to get her dog out of the park.

Final tip: If you have a big water bottle or hose handy, a splash of water in the dogs' faces will often stop a fight.

WORKOUT PERKS

....

One in three Americans is overweight, and far too many adult dogs waddle around like hairy ottomans. If you or your dog is in that group, take action together to make those excess pounds flee like fleas after a flea bath!

The benefits of exercising with your dog on a regular basis include more energy, better flexibility, fewer aches and pains, greater concentration, improved digestion, fewer doctor visits, and, most important, added years to your life and life to your years! Just make sure you check with your own doctor and with your veterinarian before starting any new exercise program.

TERRIFIC TIP

Schedule exercise before meals, not immediately after your plate and your dog's bowl are empty. You will reduce the risk of stomachaches and muscle cramps.

BOOGIE WOOGIE
BEAGLE BOY

....

Love to cha-cha with your Chihuahua or waltz with your Westie? The two of you might be ideal for a fun activity called "musical" or "canine freestyle." It involves choreographed dance moves with your canine partner. Dogs learn to spin left and right, respond to hand signals and body cues, walk on their hind legs, and take bows.

Learn more by visiting the World Canine Freestyle Organization and Canine Freestyle Federation Web sites at *www.worldcaninefreestyle.org* and *www.canine-freestyle.org*.

A FEW GOOD REASONS *to* EXERCISE *with* YOUR DOG

- Spending more time with your dog enhances the bond between you.

- Your dog is always happy to join you and won't make lame excuses.

- Running or walking together is the perfect opportunity to reinforce obedience cues and improve your communication.

- Exercise reduces the chance of your dog doing misdeeds out of boredom and lack of an appropriate energy outlet.

- You might make some new friends of both species.

There's a reason a favorite yoga pose is called "downward-facing dog." Do as your dog does by kneeling on all fours on a mat. With your hands a few inches in front of your shoulders and your palms on the ground, straighten your legs and lift your butt up, pushing strongly into your hands. Your tailbone is higher than your hips.

Now push your hands against the ground as you stretch your shoulders, keeping your neck relaxed. Breathe through your nose. Take five deep breaths and then return to your hands-and-knees position.

Build the duration and intensity of the exercise activity gradually. Don't expect your dog to chase a Frisbee nonstop for an hour on his introduction to this sport. That would be like asking you to run a mini-marathon immediately after buying your first pair of running shoes.

Treat your dog to a warm-up stretch before jogging or other high-energy activity. Use a treat to lure your dog into a play bow (outstretched front legs, head low, rear end up high) in order to s-t-r-e-t-c-h her front muscles. Have her lie on her side while you gently but firmly stretch each limb, one at a time, holding each stretch for five to ten seconds before releasing. Finish by having your dog turn in a circle a few times or weave in and out of your legs to finish limbering up.

NICE CATCH!

....

Some dogs are naturals at fetching Frisbees. Find out by tossing a disk into the air and noting if your dog follows it with his eyes — that's a good sign. Start off by engaging him in a friendly game of fetch with a small floppy disk made of nylon or canvas especially for dogs. Praise and repeat. Your goal is to have your dog chase, catch, and return the disk consistently.

If you can hurl a Frisbee with accuracy and your dog loves to fetch, consider formal training to compete in sanctioned canine disk events. Your dog doesn't care how far you can throw as long as he can catch it. And what makes a disk catchable? Consistent distance, speed, and spin, and plenty of "air time" give your dog time to chase down this airborne object.

TERRIFIC TIP

When you want to practice your
tennis serve, bring your ball-happy
dog to the enclosed courts (if dogs are
allowed). You can work on your lobs
and slams while your dog gets
a workout fetching and retrieving
the tennis balls.

PLAY BALL!

....

If your dog is a retrieving fool, he might fare fine in a sport called "flyball." This organized sport is ideal for high-energy, ball-crazy dogs who love to sprint and jump. Herding and retrieving breeds really love this sport.

Each team consists of four dogs and their handlers. The goal is for each dog to race down a 51-foot course, leap over four hurdles, hit a pedal to release a ball into the air, snag the ball, and charge back to the starting line. A good team can complete their entire run in about 20 seconds.

Find more details at the North American Flyball Association Web site at *www.flyball.org*.

Does your dog have springs in his legs? Encourage his hurdling talents by installing a low baby gate across a doorway in your house. For a small dog, try a piece of plank that is 30 or 36 inches long and 8, 10, or 12 inches wide (or high, since you are placing the plank on its side across the doorway).

When your dog is sitting on one side of the barrier, lure him up and over by tossing a treat or his favorite toy to the other side for him to fetch. This is good aerobic exercise; just be careful not to overdo it.

You'll not find a more reliable running mate than your dog. He won't brush you off because he either partied too late the night before or he'd rather watch TV. To pamper your canine jogger and keep him in great shape:

- Check with your veterinarian to make sure your dog is up to the challenge and condition the dog gradually.

- Use a leather leash. It's easier to grip and won't cut into your hand the way nylon can.

- Keep your dog at your side; if he tries to cut in front of you, extend your leg in front of him.

- For jogs longer than 20 minutes, put a lightweight pack on your dog to hold his water supply. Stash a few plastic bags to scoop up any poop.

- Run on grass whenever possible to cushion your dog's feet and joints and protect his pads.

- Don't take your dog with you in extremely warm or cold weather.

- Check your dog's paws for any signs of cuts or injuries after each jog.

- Use safety lights and reflective tape for nighttime jaunts.

As you try to teach your dog any athletic sport, such as agility or flyball, be sure to display your excitement and enthusiasm. Your upbeat attitude is contagious to your canine. Before a training session or a class, motivate your dog with a fun activity, like a quick game of tug to get him ready to focus on you and bring out his true canine jock.

TERRIFIC TIP

To prepare your dog for advanced training, take a small treat in your hand and have your dog play follow-the-treat. Say "watch me" or "pay attention" and reward him for keeping his eyes glued to you.

Before you sign up for a new canine sport, size up your dog's energy level, attention span, and ability to cope with distractions. These are keys to help you to decide if he can succeed in an organized event.

Think about how to bring out the athletic best in your dog. In general, long-legged, light-framed dogs such as Jack Russells and springer spaniels are best suited for leaping and long-distance running. Short-legged, stocky-framed canines such as corgis and dachshunds tend to fare best in activities involving short energy bursts or steady-paced walks.

Know and honor your dog's personality and drive. You may have visions of your dog becoming the best agility dog in your zip code, but he might prefer competing in flyball or leaping off a dock into the water.

THE DOG "DECATHLON"

....

Agility competitions are a true test of a dog's athletic ability and his bond with the handler. Contestants run through timed obstacle courses featuring hurdles, teeter-totters, steep inclines, tires, weave poles, tunnels, and walkways. Dogs must pay close attention to hand signals, eye contact, and other cues to navigate successfully. The great thing about agility is that dogs of all shapes and sizes can excel.

Here are the four main national agility organizations:

- American Kennel Club for purebreds (*www.akc.org*)
- North American Dog Agility Council (*www.nadac.com*)
- United Kennel Club (*www.ukcdogs.com*)
- United States Dog Agility Association (*www.usdaa.com*)

Turn your backyard into a mini-agility course without taking a bite out of your budget. Construct hurdles using PVC pipes and screws. Use a row of toilet plungers or four-foot-high garden stakes in the lawn as weave poles. Instead of a hanging tire, tie a hula hoop to a couple of stakes or sandwich it between a pair of laundry baskets for your dog to leap through. A kiddy play tunnel works well for most dogs. Just make sure that all obstacles are sturdy and won't tip over or come crashing down on your dog — that would dampen his enthusiasm for this fun activity!

E-x-t-e-n-d walks with your dogs on days when the weather is inviting and you both feel frisky and up for a solid workout. Instead of walking or running the same old route, hop into the car and visit a dog-friendly county park, climb a nearby mountain, or find a new jogging trail in the woods or along a river or lake. You'll both enjoy the change of scenery. In between brisk paces, allow your dog to stop and sniff her surroundings.

Water-loving dogs enjoy a new sport called "dock diving," which first aired on ESPN in 2000. Think of this as an aquatic long jump. The dog leaps off a dock, goes airborne, and hits the water in pursuit of a toy flung by the handler. The length of the jump is measured from the edge of the dock to the point where the dog's rear end breaks the water — minus the tail. To learn more, visit *www.splashdogs.com*.

TERRIFIC TIP

Know when to call it quits and always end before your dog becomes exhausted. One clue: An overexerted dog will display a "spade tongue" — red, wide, and dry — a sign of dehydration.

JUMP RIGHT IN!

....

Do you live with a canine version of Olympian Mark Spitz? Swimming is great exercise because it works all the muscle groups without jarring the joints. Have your water-loving dog fetch a floatable toy or a stick.

Be sure to check out the cleanliness of the body of water, and keep tabs on the currents if you're playing in a river or the ocean. For a backyard pool, install a ramp or steps so that your dog has an easy and safe way to get in and out, and show him where it is.

Consider your dog's overall health and age when you allow him to make a splash. Older dogs will tucker out sooner than younger ones and will also become chilled faster.

Whatever activity you choose, remember that you're only human and that your dog is not perfect. Mistakes happen. Don't blame your dog for any miscues. Instead, work on improving your communication with your canine — both verbal and hand signals.

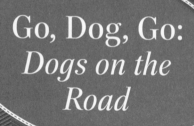

Go, Dog, Go: *Dogs on the Road*

HAPPY DOG
HAPPY YO

Chapter
Seven

WE ARE BOMBARDED BY STATISTICS EVERY DAY, BUT HERE'S ONE FACT I LOVE TO BARK about: More than 29 million dogs travel with their pet parents each year in North America. Recognizing this trend, hotels from budget to five-star, as well as vacation destinations such as canine camps and pet-friendly parks, are putting out the welcome mat for dogs. So pack your bags and delight your road rover with these magical words: "Hey, do you want to go on a trip?" Here are some fun places to go as well as tips for happy (and safe) trails.

Splurge on your dog's birthday or other red-letter day by booking a stay at a hotel that has truly gone to the dogs. Pet-friendly amenities may include oversized pillows, plush doggy robes, check-in gift packages with toys and treats, canine room service menus, and even a licensed dog masseuse. Some fancy hotels offer dog-walking services operated by staff wearing white gloves and packing plenty of disposal bags.

You've heard it before, but never leave your dog inside the car — at any time of year, but especially in the hot summer — for even a few minutes. On a relatively balmy day with temperatures in the 60s, the interior of a car can quickly heat up to an uncomfortable 90°F or even higher in the sun.

Leaving the windows open a crack is no guarantee against heatstroke. Your dog could become severely sick or even die. Some newer vehicles feature a remote ignition that allows you to keep the air conditioning on inside a locked car while you dash into a store.

TERRIFIC TIP

Dogs perspire through their footpads. On long, hot rides, spritz your dog's paws with a spray bottle of water for a real cooldown. You can also carry a wet washcloth in a plastic bag to cool down your canine.

Buckle up your basset hound and secure your Sheltie. An unrestrained 60-pound dog in a 30-mph crash can generate an impact force of 1,200 pounds against the windshield, seat back, or people! Use a harness with a dog seat belt, keep your dog in a crate, or secure him in the back of the car behind a floor-to-ceiling metal frame. These options ensure a safer ride for you and your dog.

ROGER THAT, ROVER

....

Resist the temptation to let your dog stick her face out the car window. Flying debris could injure her eyes or ears. Lower the window only enough to keep the air flowing. If your dog insists on poking her head out the window, strap on some safety goggles designed for dogs. She'll truly look the part of copilot!

HOLD *the* FRIES

....

Keep a stash of healthy road treats tucked in the glove compartment or in a small cooler. When you stop at a drive-through window, treat your dog to nutritious biscuits, carrot sticks, or apple slices instead of buying her a burger.

It's okay to give her a small piece of meat, or better yet, just let her lick your greasy fingers after you're done, but cooked fat is hard for dogs to digest. Too much of it puts your dog at risk for pancreatitis, not to mention obesity and all the problems that go with it, such as diabetes and liver and heart disease.

Before hopping into the car for a long road trip, contact the Department of Tourism for each state you plan to visit. The phone numbers for each capital city are available from directory assistance or on the Internet. The agencies can help you find pet-accepting vacation spots and hotels. You can also solicit the help of a travel agent, or, if you're a member of the American Automobile Association, your local chapter can assist you.

And you can fetch info off the Internet from any of these helpful dog travel sites:

- *www.fidofriendly.com*
- *www.bringfido.com*
- *www.takeyourpet.com*
- *www.petsonthego.com*
- *www.dogfriendly.com*

TERRIFIC TIP

Train your dog to heed the "wait" command, especially when you open your vehicle's door or hatch. Attach a leash before letting him out of the car to prevent escapes or accidents.

TAIL WAGS *for* TECHNOLOGY

....

Nowadays, finding a pet-friendly destination is a simple cell phone call away. Access to thousands of dog-pleasing places, such as outdoor dining, dog beaches, parks, campgrounds, hotels, and off-leash dog parks, plus info like airline travel policies, toll-free emergency numbers, and more is now available with just a few clicks on a mobile phone. Check it out at *www.go2pets.com.*

Hmmm...where would your dog like to visit? Why not state parks? These natural wonderlands provide plenty of spots for walking and hiking. Or head for national parks. Many of them, including Yellowstone and the Mall in Washington, D.C., permit leashed dog visitors. Start by searching the National Park Service at *www.nps.gov* for general information, and then contact the particular park that you are considering visiting to check on their pet policy.

If the only time your dog rides in the car is to visit the veterinarian, it's no wonder he begins to whimper and hide under the bed the minute you jingle your car keys. Ninety-nine percent of car rides should be fun for your dog. You may not be able to make him beg to go for a checkup, but you can make him happier about hopping into the car.

Work your way up to longer trips by taking your dog on frequent short trips. Start with trips to dog-pleasing places: dog parks, the beach, Grandma's house, or the biscuit-delivering teller at your drive-through bank window. Your dog will soon forget about the vet and start to associate good events with the car. Short trips also help you to determine how your dog behaves inside a car and if he is prone to motion sickness, which often subsides after puppyhood.

HOTEL TIPS

....

Practice proper pet-iquette while traveling with your canine mate. Take only house-trained dogs to a hotel, and don't attempt to sneak your dog in. There are many reasons for the pet ban at certain hotels, including the welfare of guests who have allergies.

- Always give your dog a good walk before you check in to prevent any accidental puddles and to drain some rambunctious energy.

- Check with a concierge in advance about pet-sitting or dog-walking services and doggy day care operations nearby so that your dog will be supervised while you go out for a leisurely dinner or to visit a museum.

- Request a ground floor room near a grassy area or other dog-beckoning surface so that you can walk your dog without a lot of hassles. Toss a couple of poop bags into your pocket and scout out the nearest trash can so that you can practice good guest etiquette.

- Never leave your dog alone in the hotel room. He may bark, chew, or dig holes in the carpet.

- Keep a "dog inside" sign posted on the outside of your door — above and beyond the "privacy please" signs.

- Tip the housekeeper well. There will be a little extra work involved in de-dogging the room after you depart, especially if you have a super shedder or a drooler.

ON *the* ROAD

....

Carry water and a bowl for your dog, even on short rides. A quick trip can sometimes unexpectedly become a long journey. Pack water in resealable plastic containers and stash them in a place out of direct sunlight.

Give your dog a brightly colored bandana with her name on it for easy identification (if you become separated, it will make it easier for dog-friendly people to call her by name) and a harness you can grab onto during an emergency situation. Make a fun to-do about the new clothing to make her feel pampered and pleased.

On long rides, stop every two or three hours for potty breaks and to stretch. Many highway rest stops provide posted areas for dogs to "take care of business." Don't forget to go on poop patrol.

TERRIFIC TIP

Pack your dog's favorite blanket or
bedding to make her feel more at home
in a strange hotel room. Add a bed
sheet or light blanket to cover the hotel
bed if your dog is allowed to snooze
with you.

READ *the* FINE PRINT

....

One way to turn a smile upside down is to be caught by surprise, especially in the pocketbook. Check the hotel's pet policy carefully. Some places charge nonrefundable fees that can go as high as $150 per night for canine guests.

Enjoy all the creature comforts of a home-away-from-home by booking travel at time-shares, cabins, or vacation rentals that accept well-mannered pets. You and your dog can stay in a spacious place with plenty of amenities. Some places even include maid service and fenced areas for safe romping.

Camping with dogs is pleasurable whether it's an overnight stay or a two-week adventure in the backcountry. This activity traces its roots back centuries to when humans and dogs hunted for food together and shared campfires. Fresh air and new sights, sounds, and smells await your pooch, not to mention swimming and splashing in lakes and rivers. Consider your dog's size, age, health, and attitude when deciding on a camping adventure so that it is fun for both of you.

A PACK *for* YOUR POOCH

....

In-shape dogs can sport canine-style backpacks to lessen your load during daylong or overnight hikes. A properly fitted backpack places the weight over a dog's shoulders, not in the middle of the back.

Select a model that is lightweight and waterproof, offers padding to prevent rubbing, and features adjustable straps and quick-snap buckles.

Go for color by choosing a backpack that is bright red, orange, or yellow so it can be easily spotted in the woods if your dog is off-leash and runs ahead of you.

Try it out near home to check for chafing or slipping before heading out for any long hikes.

Did you love summer camp as a kid? What about going back to camp but being able to bring your best friend with you? There are dozens of canine camps around the country that provide the opportunity to spend some real quality time with your dog. Some camps offer specific programs while others just let you hang out with your pal and other like-minded dog lovers.

You can learn new training techniques (ever tried clicker training?), investigate new activities (what's agility all about, anyway?), or hone an existing skill (take your hound for a tracking tune-up).

Locate dog camps near you by visiting:

www.dogpatch.org/doginfo/camp.html.

Bring out the true dog paddler in your canine pal by enjoying a guided canoe trip on lakes and rivers through-out North America. Nothing beats skimming the calm waters with your dog as First Mate. To learn more about canine canoe trips, contact Dog Paddling Adventures in Ontario, Canada, at *www.dogpaddlingadventures.com.*

For sure-footed, water-loving dogs, kayaking can be a memorable adventure. If you love to kayak and want to include your dog, consider buying your own kayak. Select a two-person model with an open-board design that can accommodate most dogs. Apply a nonslip rubber surface available at boating stores to the top so your dog will be able to ride in style without slipping off.

If you are renting a kayak, call ahead to make sure the rental place permits dogs. Whether you are planning a quick jaunt or a long outing, always have your dog in a life jacket and bring a leash, harness, and treats inside a waterproof bag, bottled water, first-aid kit, sunscreen, and floating toys if your dog loves to fetch.

Admire your dog enough to make him, say, an admiral? Go first class on the water by booking a trip on a dog-friendly houseboat. These floating vacations provide you and your dog the chance to enjoy calm waters in beautiful places. You can choose to stay safely anchored or to travel peacefully down a river or canal.

Tips: Take plenty of towels to wipe off muddy paws, doggy life jackets, and a "portable dog potty" for times when you aren't able to dock on shore. When your dog returns from romping on land, check his paws for cuts and his body for any foxtails or burrs.

FLYING *the* FRIENDLY SKIES

....

In our post-9/11 world, airline rules are constantly evolving. Get the scoop on the latest pet policies by visiting the airline's Web site directly. Here are some general tips:

- Help pilot a happy takeoff and smooth landing by booking a nonstop flight.

- Always travel on the same flight as your dog.

- Make sure you know what documentation is required for a flight. Have extra copies of your dog's up-to-date health records and inoculations.

- You can never have too much identification
  when it comes to your airborne dog! Put detailed
  contact information on his collar and paste it to
  his crate where he cannot get at it. Include travel
  phone numbers.

- Bring a current photograph of your dog with you.
  If he gets lost in the airport or at the destination,
  the photograph can make the search go much more
  smoothly.

- Book early. Most airlines make pet reservations on a
  first-come, first-served basis.

- A dog who weighs under 15 pounds may be able to ride
  with you in the passenger section on some airlines.

- Avoid flying during holidays when there is a greater
  chance for flight delays and cancellations.

Check out the PetTravel Web site (*www.pettravel.com*), which boasts of providing the Internet's most complete source of information for traveling with your pet anywhere in the world by car, train, or air.

Tail-wagging Extras

Chapter Eight

HAPPY DOG
HAPPY YOU

....

HOW DO WE LOVE OUR DOGS? LET ME COUNT THE WAGS. NOTHING CONVEYS PURE JOY LIKE THE thump, thump, thump of a happy dog's tail. What's the best gift you can give your dog? Time — as in spending quality minutes, hours, and days with your canine companion. This final chapter addresses some extra ways for you to show how much you care for that special tail-wagger of yours.

....

FILE *under* "P" *for* PREPARED

....

Create a file folder for each of your pets. Include medical records, current photos, microchip ID number, and the names and contact information of pet sitters, boarding centers, and doggy day-care centers. Describe your pet's personality—both endearing traits and challenging habits — plus his eating schedule and favorite treats.

Stash any special awards or achievements, such as acing an agility level or earning Canine Good Citizenship status, in this folder, too. This file comes in handy when you need to visit the veterinary clinic, hire a pet sitter, qualify for an advanced competition, or initiate a search if your dog ever becomes lost.

If your beloved pal is a former pound puppy, occasionally buy an extra bag of treats, a toy, or a dog bed and donate these items to the animal shelter where you adopted him. Most shelters have lists of supplies they need as well as many opportunities to volunteer. It's a great way to help other dogs in need of loving homes and to remind yourself of how glad you are to have found your own dog.

TOO MUCH TOGETHERNESS?

....

If your dog is a pillow hog and you want him to start sleeping in his own bed, start by buying a cushy, comfy foam doggy bed and putting it in your bedroom. Wash the cover and tuck it between your bedspread and top sheet. Let it remain there a few days to collect your scent, and then put the cover back and lure your dog to the bed with a treat or favorite toy.

Reward him for spending time there and patiently take him back to his new bed every time he comes begging to jump up and snuggle with you. It may take some time and patience, but in the end he will learn to love his new snoozing spot — after all, he's still right near his favorite person.

TAKE THIS JOB *and* SHARE IT

....

Convince your boss and coworkers to participate in the annual Take Your Dog to Work Day or, better yet, expand the company policy to permit well-behaved pets in the workplace every day. About a decade ago, Pet Sitters International created Take Your Dog To Work Day, which is always held in late June.

I love the event's motto: "It's the 'leash' you can do." TYDTW Day does more than give you the chance to show off your well-behaved pup. It also breeds awareness in coworkers of just how doggone grrr-eat dogs can be — and that helps increase adoptions at animal shelters.

Well-mannered, people-pleasing dogs give us comfort and teach us to take breaks (for play, not coffee). According to a recent survey conducted by the American Association of Pet Product Manufacturers (which you should share with your productivity-minded boss), here are some "bone fide" benefits of dogs in the workplace:

- 55 million Americans believe that having pets in the workplace leads to a more creative environment.

- 53 million Americans believe that having pets in the workplace decreases absenteeism.

- 50 million Americans believe that having pets in the workplace helps coworkers to get along better.

- 38 million Americans believe that having pets in the workplace creates a more productive work environment.

- 46 million Americans who take their pets to the workplace say that they work longer hours.

Here are some keys to creating a successful pet-welcoming policy at your workplace:

- Emphasize to coworkers that only dogs capable of lying quietly and not barking at strangers should be granted workplace privileges.

- Dog-proof the office, and particularly your work area, by tucking away electric cords and office supplies such as permanent markers or correction fluid.

- Provide a couple of toys to amuse your dog and healthy snacks in case your coworkers want to make friends by offering a treat.

- Schedule time during the day to feed and walk your dog (who will be using the outside lawn, not the executive bathroom). Keep extra poop bags in your briefcase or desk drawer.

- Bring a dog gate or crate so your dog has a safe place to hang out and cannot run loose and unsupervised in the office, and provide your dog with his own bed or blanket to snooze on.

- Never force a coworker to pet or interact with your dog. Some people are afraid or have pet allergies and others have not yet been enlightened by the magic of mutts.

I hope you never go through the trauma of losing your dog, but it can happen anytime, anywhere. A frightened dog might run away during a thunderstorm or slip out the door undetected. Dogs can be stolen right out of your backyard.

One way to provide some peace of mind is to book a date with your veterinarian to insert an identification microchip under your dog's skin, usually on the back of the neck. Many animal shelters and veterinary clinics have scanners that can be run over a stray dog's back to reveal vital contact information.

In addition to the usual posters with photo on telephone poles and calls to your local veterinarians and animal shelters, there are several services available to help reunite you with your lovable pooch if the unthinkable happens. Keep these Web sites handy:

- *www.petfinder.com*
- *www.fidofinder.com*
- *www.pets911.com*
- *www.dogdetective.com*

THE PERFECT PET SITTER

....

Sometimes we just have to leave our dogs behind when we travel. If your dog hates going to a kennel, a professional pet sitter can be the perfect solution. Have the pet sitter stop by and visit with your dog before you leave. This strategy helps your dog to feel more comfortable and reduces his anxiety level while you're gone.

For local referrals, contact the National Association of Professional Pet Sitters (NAPPS) at 800-296-PETS or *www.petsitters.org*, or Pet Sitters International (PSI) at 800-268-SITS or *www.petsit.com*.

Make your refrigerator door Dog Information Central. Post your dog's name (and nickname), how much food she eats and when she eats it, location of the food, location of and instructions for any medications, likes and dislikes, house rules, leash location, and, most important, how to contact you and your vet.

Ensure that your dog is safe and happy while you're away by providing the pet sitter with these essentials:

- Extra cash in case the food runs out

- Directions for setting the thermostat or air conditioning in case of dramatic changes in the weather

- The phone number of and directions to your regular veterinary clinic or hospital

- A list outlining potential pitfalls around the house ("Always close doors quickly because Buttons likes to try to dart outside" or "Keep the toilet lid down because Frankie is a bowl drinker")

- An introduction to a friendly neighbor before your departure (have them exchange phone numbers)

GOLDEN OLDIES

....

Never think that you're too old to enjoy the company of a canine. I have many senior friends who feel fortunate to share their homes and hearts with dogs. And many shelters offer special adoption fees for people who take a shine to a senior dog. Regardless of your age, always have a plan on how your pet will be cared for should he or she outlive you.

Is your dog a "people pooch"? Think about giving back to your community by training your dog to become a certified therapy dog. The two of you will develop a truly special relationship by reaching out to others. Together you can bring joy to hospitals and nursing homes and instill good people-pet skills in classrooms. Learn more by visiting *www.therapydogs.com.*

FURRY FUND-RAISERS

....

Looking for a way to raise money for a school event? The homeless? A local animal shelter? Why not raise funds — and awareness — by staging a dog wash, a just-for-fun dog show, or a pet parade in your community? You and your dog can serve as cochairs for these events.

For a special occasion or just because it's the weekend, here is a tasty Breakfast Bonanza that you and your dog can enjoy together:

> 1 tablespoon margarine
> 3 eggs
> 2 ham slices, diced
> 2 cheddar cheese slices

1. Heat the margarine in a nonstick skillet over medium heat.

2. Add the eggs and scramble until they are fluffy.

3. Add the ham and cheese slices and stir until well mixed.

4. Allow your dog's portion to cool before giving it to him.

For a more festive breakfast, invite a favorite canine pal and human to join you (just double up the recipe).

BE *a* GOOD CITIZEN

....

A great way to further your bond with your dog is to enroll in a Canine Good Citizen (CGC) certification program. This program teaches dogs — with pedigrees and without — manners and proper behavior for getting along with humans. Dogs must pass 10 separate tests before earning this distinction. When Chipper, my former shelter dog, aced this exam, it was difficult to tell which one of us sported the biggest grin.

Here's a quick rundown of the 10 tests for temperament and manners:

Test 1. Accept the approach of a friendly stranger while leashed and with owner.

Test 2. Sit politely for petting by a friendly stranger without any signs of shyness or resentment.

Test 3. Be clean, well groomed, and at a healthy weight, and accept brushing, handling of the paws, and examination of the ears by the test-giver.

Test 4. Walk on a leash without yanking or pulling, and respond to cues to stop or turn.

Test 5. Walk through a crowd politely without showing any signs of aggression, shyness, or overexcitement.

Test 6. Sit and down on command and stay in place until called by the owner.

Test 7. Come when called from a distance of 10 feet or more from the owner.

Test 8. Walk past another leashed dog as the two people exchange pleasantries, and not react to the other dog.

Test 9. Express natural interest and curiosity but not appear startled or panicked by distractions such as a dropped chair, a jogger running by, or a noisy wheeled crate.

Test 10. Maintain good manners when left with a trusted person as the owner moves out of eyesight for three minutes. The dog cannot show any signs of nervousness or agitation during this time of supervised separation.

For information, contact the American Kennel Club (AKC) at 919-233-9767 or on the Web at *www.akc.org*. The AKC is the umbrella organization that awards the CGC certificates.

TERRIFIC TIP

Use window stickers indicating the number of dogs (and cats) in your house to alert police or firefighters in case of an emergency. You can get these stickers from the Humane Society of the United States and possibly from your local animal shelters.

Mother Nature isn't always nice. Sometimes she unleashes wildfires, floods, earthquakes, hurricanes, and other natural disasters that force people to evacuate. Keep your dog safe by thinking ahead. Stash a crate, packed with doggy essentials and that you can quickly grab and go, in the garage or storage closet. Include a copy of your dog's medical records, spare leash, collapsible water and food bowls, food and treats in waterproof containers, first-aid kit, spares of your dog's meds, extra set of pet ID papers, can opener, plastic spoon, and yes, a muzzle. Even a loving pet might snap when frightened or highly stressed.

Protect your pet with health insurance. Monthly household budgets often overlook a potentially major drain on the family income: medical costs for our canine chums. Certain cancer treatments can cost as much as $10,000 or more, and surgeries are always expensive.

Are you financially prepared? Premiums vary among companies as well as among dogs. Typically, premiums cost less for puppies and healthy adult dogs than for senior dogs and those with already diagnosed conditions, such as allergies or cancer.

Pay heed to the insurance policy's conditions. Some do not offer coverage for preexisting conditions such as hip dysplasia. Others offer add-on riders at extra costs to deal with routine wellness exams, spaying or neutering, and dental care.

Cast a canine charm on people who feel threatened or frightened by large dogs. Resist the temptation to force an introduction between a nervous person and your sweet but huge pooch. Instead, ask your dog to perform a trick, such as a "belly up" or a "play bow," to help the person to feel less apprehensive. Or have your dog go into a pray pose or fake a faint and flop on the ground. Your dog will be happy to comply, and you might just reduce the fear and produce a smile.

Where there's a will, there's a way of life for your dog —long after you're gone. Don't run the risk of your best buddy not having a place to go in the event of your death.

Establish a pet trust that designates someone to care for your faithful dog and provides for his lifelong care after you die. You can designate a specific amount to be spent monthly or annually on your dog or leave it up to the executor's discretion. You can also specify that any unused balance of the trust money be donated to a humane society, animal shelter, or favorite animal charity.

Legal trusts can cost from $75 to $400 to set up, depending on whether you obtain the form online or work with an attorney. The benefit of a living trust is that unlike with a will, the conditions can be put into effect immediately upon your death, bypassing the time-consuming probate process.

The Humane Society of the United States (HSUS) offers a free brochure, "Planning for Your Pet's Future without You." It outlines steps to take to prepare for the unexpected and to ensure that your dog will be cared for in a safe, loving environment after you die. Call the HSUS at 202-452-1100 or visit *www.hsus.org*.

Let your dog be your guru. When it comes to displays of human kindness, it seems as though dogs win by a nose. A recent poll of dog owners by the American Pet Product Manufacturers Association asked them to count the number of times in a day their dog showed them affection as compared with the number of times in a day a friend or family member did. The result: Dogs display affection four times more often.

Tap into that loving nature and take the time to respond to your dog's wagging tail, grinning mouth, and happy-to-see-you expression. A quick pat, a minute to "shake paws," or even just a few cheerful words will make your dog's day.

Dogs are not our whole life, but
they make our lives whole.

– Roger Caras

RESOURCES

....

American Humane Association
www.americanhumane.org

American Kennel Club
www.akc.org

American Society for the
Prevention of Cruelty to
Animals
www.aspca.org

Delta Society
www.deltasociety.org

Humane Society of the
United States
www.hsus.org

Animal Behavior

Animal Behavior Network
www.animalbehavior.net

International Association of
Animal Behavior Consultants
www.iaabc.org

Association of Pet Dog Trainers
www.apdt.com

Finding Lost Pets

Dog Detective
www.dogdetective.com

Fido Finder
www.fidofinder.com

Pet Finders
www.petfinder.com

Pets 911
www.pets911.com

Pet Health and News

Animal Radio
www.animalradio.com

ASPCA Poison Control Center
888-426-4435
www.aspca.org

National Association of
Professional Pet Sitters
www.petsitters.org

Pets Best
www.petsbest.com

Pet-friendly rentals
www.rentwithpets.org

Pet Life Radio
www.petliferadio.com

Pet Relocation
www.petrelocation.com

Pet Sitters International
www.petsit.com

Canine Sports

Canine Freestyle Federation
www.canine-freestyle.org

Dock Dogs (dock jumping)
www.dockdog.com

North American Dog Agility
Council
www.nadac.com

North American Flyball
Association
www.flyball.org

United States Dog Agility
Association
www.usdaa.com

World Canine Freestyle
Organization
www.worldcaninefreestyle.org

Pet Travel

BringFido.com
www.bringfido.com

DogFriendly.com
www.dogfriendly.com
Fido Friendly Magazine
www.fidofriendly.com

Pets on the Go!
www.petsonthego.com

Takeyourpet.com
www.takeyourpet.com

Dog Paddling Adventures
www.dogpaddlingadventures.com
Dog Scouts of America
www.dogscouts.com

National Park Service
www.nps.gov

INDEX

OTHER STOREY TITLES
YOU WILL ENJOY

....

The Dog Behavior Answer Book, by Arden Moore.
Answers to your questions about canine quirks, baffling
habits, and destructive behavior.
336 pages. Paper. ISBN 978-1-58017-644-6.

Dr. Kidd's Guide to Herbal Dog Care, by Randy Kidd, DVM, PhD.
A comprehensive guide to gentle, chemical-free treatments
for your beloved canine.
208 pages. Paper. ISBN 978-1-58017-189-2.

Happy Cat, Happy You, by Arden Moore.
Hundreds of quick tips and training games for busy owners
and their feline friends.
304 pages. Paper. ISBN 978-1-60342-033-4.

The Puppy Owner's Manual, by Diana Delmar.
How to solve all your puppy problems and create a puppy-
friendly home.
192 pages. Paper. ISBN 978-1-58017-401-5.

Real Food for Dogs, by Arden Moore.
A collection of 50 vet-approved recipes to please your
canine gastronome.
128 pages. Paper. ISBN 978-1-58017-424-4.

These and other books from Storey Publishing are available
wherever quality books are sold or by calling 1-800-441-5700.
Visit us at *www.storey.com.*